The Computer Graphics Glossary

The Computer Graphics Glossary

by Stuart W. Hubbard

ORYX PRESS
1983

The rare Arabian Oryx is believed to have inspired the myth of the unicorn. This desert antelope became virtually extinct in the early 1960s. At that time several groups of international conservationists arranged to have 9 animals sent to the Phoenix Zoo to be the nucleus of a captive breeding herd. Today the Oryx population is over 400 and herds have been returned to reserves in Israel, Jordan, and Oman.

Copyright © 1983 by The Oryx Press

Published by The Oryx Press
2214 North Central at Encanto
Phoenix, AZ 85004

Published simultaneously in Canada

Printed and Bound in the United States of America

Library of Congress Cataloging in Publication Data

Hubbard, Stuart W.
   The computer graphics glossary.

   1. Computer graphics—Dictionaries.   I. Title.
T385.H78   1983   001.64'43   82-42918
ISBN 0-89774-072-6

Introduction

The Computer Graphics Glossary is a much-needed tool, useful not only to computer-aided design and computer-aided manufacturing (CAD/CAM) professionals but to those outside the industry who are intent on learning more about this flourishing technology. Therefore, it is my hope that this glossary will grow and develop as the computer graphics industry itself grows.

This book is descriptive, as are all good glossaries. It does not prescribe. This is particularly important in an industry as young and fast-paced as computer graphics where debate is bound to erupt around the usage and precise meaning of newly coined terms. Such debate is healthy and natural, but it does present challenges for the glossarist. Therefore, in those instances where there may be contention over the meaning of terms, the most common meaning is listed first, followed by the other contending definitions. In addition, usage notes are included after the definitions of many terms in the glossary. These notes are intended to provide information on the idiomatic use of terms and to steer readers away from incorrect locutions. In disputes over spelling, however, only the most frequently used form is listed in the hope that this might aid the natural standardization process in this area.

The entries in this glossary are limited to those terms which are directly pertinent to computer graphics. Many other computer and electronics terms not specifically applicable to this field have been omitted; they can be found in any good dictionary of general data processing terminology, of which there are several.

In addition to the technical terminology, the glossary contains many important CAD/CAM product names. Those products that are trademarked are noted as such, and the product's manufacturer is identified. These names are included only with the manufacturer's permission and, therefore, some significant computer graphics names are not included—any future editions of this book will have an expanded list of such product names. For more information about those manufacturers who have granted permission to include their products, readers are advised to consult *The*

Computer Graphics Marketplace edited by John Cosentino and published by The Oryx Press.

My expectation is that this glossary will never be complete. Its completion could only mean the computer graphics industry has ceased to grow or to change. A doubtful prospect. At present, the industry is evolving with such rapidity that any glossary is incomplete the moment it is printed. This glossary is no exception. I do not say this as an apology, but only to point out the promising future of the computer graphics industry and the richness of its contribution to the world of data processing.

A

abscissa. The position on a rectangular coordinate system representing the distance of a point from the y axis as measured along a line parallel to the x axis.

absolute. Pertains to measurements or units of measurement derived from a fundamental or unchanging basis. In computer graphics, that basis is usually the origin of a coordinate system.

absolute address. 1. In computer hardware, the physical storage location of a byte of data. 2. The nomenclature used to refer to a specific, physical storage location.

absolute coordinates. The value of a location on the x, y, and z axes with respect to the origin of the coordinate system.

absolute dimension. A measure of spatial extent expressed with respect to the fixed origin of a specific coordinate system.

absolute system. A method of implementing numerical control or other computer graphics functions in which all coordinate locations are dimensioned and programed from a fixed point of origin.

absolute vector. A line segment in which the end points have been defined in relation to a designated origin point.

absolute zero point. The origin of a coordinate system. In machine tooling, the origin point for all machine axes.

acceleration. The rate of a change in velocity with respect to time. In CAD/CAM systems this applies to the feed rate of magnetic or paper tapes, the movement of a plotter pen, and the action of numerically controlled machine tools.

acceleration distance. The distance required along an axis of motion for a piece of hardware to reach optimal operating speed.

acceleration time. The amount of time required for a hardware mechanism to go from a start to standard operating speed. In graphics systems it usually applies to peripheral input/output devices.

acceptance test. A test evaluating the conformance of hardware or software to predetermined specifications. The test is often specified in the sales contract between graphics system customers and vendors, and payment is contingent upon the system passing the test.

access. Refers to the methods of handling data by which a system user can transfer information between main memory and input/output devices.

access time. The interval between the moment data are called from memory and the moment transmission is completed to the calling device. This interval is most often used when describing transmissions to a display device, i.e., cathode-ray tube screen.

active storage. Either core memory or intelligent terminal memory that contains the data currently being acted upon; data that have not been stored in the system on a permanent medium.

ADAPT (ADapted Automatically Programed Tools). A subset of the numerical control machining language APT which is especially useful for intermediate contouring functions.

Adapted Automatically Programed Tools. *See* ADAPT.

adaptive control. A method of optimizing machine tool operations by means of machine monitoring units which speed up or slow down machining operations according to what is most efficient. The control units derive the information necessary to calculate optimal machine speeds from a series of sensors which measure time and distance requirements during the whole of the machining process.

address. A coded identification, usually numerical, designating a specific location in memory, such as a register. More generally, it may refer to any name, label, or number identifying any data source or destination anywhere in a computer system.

addressable horizontal positions. Refers to all of the physical positions on which a vertical line can be written by a graphics system to a raster cathode-ray tube screen.

addressable point. Any position on a graphics input/output device that can be specified by coordinates.

addressable vertical positions. Refers to all of the physical positions on which a horizontal line can be written by a graphics system to a raster cathode-ray tube screen.

AD/380. A computer graphics system produced by Auto-trol Technology Corporation and consisting of a Sperry Univac V/77 computer, GS-1000 graphics software, graphics workstations, and optional equipment.

AEC (Architecture, Engineering, and Construction). Describes an industry segment that is one of the major markets for CAD/CAM systems. Specialized applications designed for use in this market include software for plant design, piping, electrical wiring, architectural drafting, and facilities management, among others.

aiming circle. The area of light projected onto the surface of an input/output device by a light pen. It serves to guide the user in accurately positioning the pen or in defining the area in which the pen is active.

algorithm. A term often used in computer programing to describe the method of problem solving by which solutions are derived from a prescribed set of well-defined steps of a finite number. Any step-by-step procedure for arriving at a solution to a specific problem.

aliasing. The visual effect that occurs on a display screen whenever the degree of detail in the displayed image exceeds the resolution available on the output device. This effect is sometimes described as "stair stepping" because lines appear to be broken or crooked.

allocate. Dedicating a hardware or software resource to perform a specified computing task.

alphanumeric. Nominally refers to all the characters in the standard alphabet plus the numerals 0–9. However, in computing it refers also to all the punctuation marks, mathematical symbols, and conventional symbols found on a system keyboard.

alphanumeric device. An input or input/output device with a keyboard capable of transmitting the alphanumeric character set. If the device has display capabilities, characters are formed in a cell matrix or as vector-generated graphics data.

American Standard Code for Information Interchange. *See* ASCII.

analog. Refers to the representation of data as continuously varying physical quantities. An analog computer represents data by physical magnitudes in electrical signals.

analysis. The calculation of engineering or geometric properties by a computer graphics system.

analytical modeling. The process of representing physical qualities (length, width, density, weight, curvatures, etc.) mathematically. It is used extensively in computer-aided manufacturing by engineers and designers who are formulating new product plans. The advent of 32-bit architecture has made analytical modeling easier, more accurate, and, therefore, more prevalent in recent years.

ancestral relation. Describes the dependency of a graphics file or entity upon some previously defined entity such as a directory file.

annotation. A critical, explanatory, or descriptive textual note associated with a graphics entity in a graphics system database.

antialiasing. Any process intended to reduce the distracting visual effects of aliasing; stair-step lines are made to appear straight and unbroken.

appearance. The visible aspect of graphic data as it is output from a computer graphics system. Usually refers to such attributes as resolution, intensity, and color.

application. A set of tasks that must be accomplished as part of a CAD/CAM enterprise. An application may consist of manual procedures, computerized procedures, or both.

application software. A set of programs written to satisfy the work requirements of a specific job or industry. In computer graphics such jobs as circuit design, cartography, piping layouts, and facilities management are commonly addressed by application software. These groups of programs, often termed "application packages," are usually sold by vendors as options to standard CAD/CAM systems.

APT (Automatically Programed Tool). An artificial language consisting of English language statements that describe the visual qualities of an engineering drawing produced on a CAD/CAM system. A sequence of APT statements is commonly used to define the geometry of a machined part which can then be produced with a tool cutter that may be controlled by a numerical control computer-aided manufacturing system.

arc. A segment of a circle or ellipse generated on a graphics system by the simultaneous, coordinated motion of two or three axes. Arcs are described as clockwise or counterclockwise depending on the direction of their movement with respect to the perpendicular axis in the plane of motion.

architecture. The general method of design and construction of a computer system. Often it refers specifically to the hardware makeup of the central processing unit and the size of the byte it processes, e.g., 16-bit architecture, 32-bit architecture. The general trend in CAD/CAM systems is toward 32-bit architecture, which is often faster and more accurate than 16-bit processing.

architecture, engineering, and construction. *See* AEC.

archives. Refers to copies of on-line data files kept off-line for use as historical records or as safeguards against the accidental loss of the on-line data.

argument. Refers to all the optional and required symbols or terms that may follow a graphics command entered on the command line of a graphics system. These command elements allow the user to more closely define the processing operation being executed.

arithmetic element. The part of APT software that calculates, within specified tolerances, the machine cutter positions of a numerically controlled device.

arithmetic operations. In computer processing, any of the binary functions of addition, subtraction, multiplication, and division or either of the unary functions of negation and absolute valuation.

array. Any organized arrangement of related graphic elements in a graphics file.

array explode. Any procedure designed to extract data from a graphics array.

artificial intelligence. Refers to the capabilities of a computer system which are more usually associated with human intelligence. Applies especially to highly interactive systems, such as CAD/CAM systems, in which the computer is programed to simulate the qualities of judgement, reason, and learning, thus making the operation of the system more accessible to noncomputer professionals.

artificial language. A system of communication based on a finite set of prescribed rules established prior to its first use. Programing languages are artificial languages.

Artwork Generation System. A device that produces film or glass plate artwork masters by using a plotter table, an optical exposure head with light source, and a plotter control. Such a device is manufactured by Gerber Scientific Instrument Company.

Artwork Generation System. Produces artwork masters on film or glass plate.

ASCII (American Standard Code for Information Interchange). A system for representing the full alphanumeric character set in 8-bit form which has been accepted by the American Standards Association. The intent is to standardize the computerized transmission of data to achieve compatibility among all data processing systems.

aspect ratio. The ratio between the height and width of a graphics object. It is most often used to describe stroked text.

assembly. A set of mechanical parts that make a complete product when put together. In a graphics system each assembly designed on-line is often stored in its own graphics file.

assembly drawing. A graphics file representing a group of product parts forming a complete product.

assembly parts list. Refers to all the parts or subassemblies required to complete a particular assembly. On graphics systems the list is often compiled automatically during the design process by the bill of material application software.

associate dimensioning. The automatic updating of dimension information related to specific graphic entities as those entities are edited, scaled, or otherwise altered.

Associated Properties Processor. A product developed by Gerber Systems Technology, Inc. which enables its CAD/CAM systems to identify and capture nongraphic on-line data for the generation of reports or bills of material.

associativity. A logical concept by which graphic entities are joined or connected within a larger graphics data base. It permits groups of data to be processed together as a result of their logical association. Associativity is a very valuable tool for many applications including bill of material, facilities management, and database management.

asynchronous. Describes processing in which the speed of operation is not related to any timing frequency in the system but to the reception of a signal denoting the completion of the previous operation. When transmitting, as over communication lines, asynchronous data are sent a character at a time, each of which is synchronized individually.

attribute. Any characteristic of a specified group of data or byte of data including such things as name, format, record length, disk identifier, creation date, etc.

attribute management. The process of creating, determining, or deleting attributes from a graphics data base.

Auto-graph. A low-cost CAD/CAM system manufactured by Gerber Systems Technology, Inc. with software for mechanical design, detail drafting, finite element modeling, and numerical control tool path generation in two-, three-, four-, and five-axis configurations.

Auto-graph. A stand-alone Auto-graph CAD/CAM system.

automated controls. Refers to the preprogramed operation of a peripheral device by a graphics system. The controlled device automatically calculates dimensions, correlates them with the task requirements, and is directed to perform appropriate actions. Applies to machine tools, plotters, etc.

Automated Drafting System. The name given to a series of computer graphics systems manufactured by Gerber Scientific Instrument Company.

Automated Film Prep System. An electronic stripping tool that automates film preparation tasks.

Automated Drafting System. The 6242 Automated Drafting System with superplotter.

Automated Film Prep System. A system manufactured by Gerber Scientific Instrument Company which is an electronic stripping tool that automates such film preparation tasks as preparing master grids, cutting windows, scribing rules. It is made specifically for use in the graphic arts industry.

automatic drafting. The generation of drawings on a graphics system using on-line graphics database information.

automatic max-min. A procedure for determining the lower left and upper right graphics extrema of a file so that the drawing can be scaled for display on cathode-ray tube or other output device.

automatic scaling. A procedure that enlarges or reduces a graphics file to ensure that the drawing uses all of the available output area.

Automatically Programed Tool. *See* APT.

Autopart.℠ The name given to the family-of-parts software package manufactured by Gerber Systems Technology, Inc. It allows users to create a library of base parts associated by specified parameters from which new product designs can be created.

Autopath.℠ The name of a placement and routing program manufactured by Gerber Systems Technology, Inc. for use in the preparation of printed circuit boards.

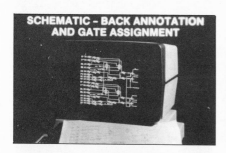
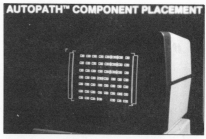
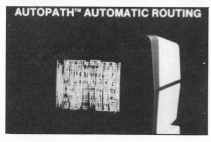
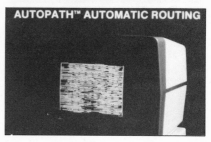

Autopath.℠ An automatic placement and routing program for preparing printed circuit boards.

Autopost.℠ A generic graphics system postprocessor manufactured by Gerber Systems Technology, Inc.

Auto-Routed. A product of Vectron Graphics System Inc. which routes traces over printed circuit boards by computer using special routing algorithms.

auxiliary operations. Any processing on a graphics system which involves peripheral devices and does not require use of the central processing unit. The processing unit is thus free to do other simultaneous work.

auxiliary storage. Refers to all data storage other than that in core memory. This includes all disk storage, tape storage, or virtual storage.

auxiliary view. A graphics entity displayed from a perspective defined by the operator rather than by some default parameter.

axis. 1. One of the straight reference lines of a two- or three-dimensional coordinate system. 2. A line of motion used in the operation of a graphics device.

B

back annotation. The extraction of information for use in making textual notes about a graphics entity after that entity has been entered in the graphics data base.

background processing. 1. Computing functions conducted without the overt knowledge of the operator. 2. Functions enacted only when the central processing unit is not occupied with jobs of higher priority.

backspace. 1. Moving the cursor one or more positions in reverse for the purpose of fixing an entry error on the command line. 2. In graphics display, the process of removing the last entered portion of graphics data, thus restoring the figure to a previous state. Used in design and engineering drafting to correct errors.

back-up. Describes an off-line copy of a file or group of files kept for reference in the event the original file or files are damaged or lost.
Usage: When used as a verb, e.g., ''I am going to back up the files,'' it is written as two words.

balloon. A circle containing descriptive data (usually text) connected to a reference location in a graphics file by a line. Commonly used in the production of diagrams.

base. 1. The side of a geometric drawing from which an altitude is drawn or measured. 2. In numbering systems, the number that is revised to various powers to generate principal counting units (decimal numbers are said to be base ten, octal numbers base eight, binary base two, etc.).

basis. The set of mathematical equations from which the form of a curve or curved surface is derived on a graphics system.

batch processing. Describes the technique of introducing into a computer system a group of programing tasks such that all tasks are conducted consecutively. The jobs are thus handled one at a time until all have been completed. This contrasts with "time sharing" wherein the user has immediate access to system processing by simultaneously sharing system resources with other users.

baud rate. A unit of electronic signaling speed equal to the number of discrete signals transmitted or received in one second. The standard baud rate for many graphics system peripherals is 9600.

benchmark. A reference point from which measurements can be made for comparison. Graphics system customers commonly have a number of vendors conduct a "benchmark problem" from which the customers can make comparisons of the speed and accuracy of the various systems before a purchase is made.

bicubic. A two-dimensional representation of a cubic shape in which the surface is defined using cubic basis functions.

bill of material. A software application often employed on graphics systems that lists all parts and materials in a product and the quantity of each. The list is then automatically updated as the product is redesigned or altered.

binary. 1. Characterized by two different parts. 2. A numbering system having two as its base. All computer processing is based on binary decisions usually expressed either as "zero" and "one" or "yes" and "no."

bit. Acronym of "binary digit." The smallest unit of information in a computer system. Usually represented by one (1) and zero (0).

bit pad. Any small digitizer designed for use on a desk top or other small work surface.

Bit Pad One.™ A low-cost digitizer for cathode-ray tube cursor control, data entry, and graphics input applications manufactured by Summagraphics Corporation.

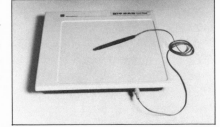

Bit Pad One.™ A standard digitizer for data entry and cursor control.

bit string. A group of arbitrarily arranged binary digits.

black box. 1. A processing system in which only the input and output data are observable. 2. A device in which the method of operation is unknown but outputs are still predictable if based on knowledge of the inputs.

blackness. The degree of intensity with which data are displayed on a cathode-ray tube. This measure is often represented by a percentage of extreme lightness or darkness.

blank. In a graphics system occurs when the electron beam of a cathode-ray tube is off and no display is visible.

blank region. A defined area of display surface within which displayed data are not visible.

blank vector. Occurs when the electron beam is blanked, resulting in a line with zero intensity. An invisible line generated on a graphics system.

blanking. The suppression of the display of graphic data or graphic layers within a drawing. This results in less data being processed and faster and more efficient displays.

blinking. Refers to the electron beam of a graphics display device which is alternately blanked and unblanked at a fixed rate. Blinking in this manner on a workstation cathode-ray tube is a technique commonly used in computer graphics to make a displayed item more apparent to the user.

block diagram. Refers to the method of reducing a problem or a system to a series of distinct, interrelated entities. The entities are represented by geometric shapes called blocks which illustrate the relationships among the parts. Often used when addressing a graphics design or engineering problem.

bootstrapping. Refers to a machine-level software routine the first few instructions of which are sufficient to bring either the rest of the routine or some other, larger program into the central processing unit from an input device. For example, a bootstrap routine is often used to facilitate system start-up.

bounding box. A rectangle with dimensions that enable it to surround a specified graphics entity. Often such rectangles are constructed to be as small as possible while still completely surrounding the object.

branching. A point in the execution of a routine where a choice in the direction of the processing must be made. This is a common occurrence in menu-driven mechanical design software systems. Based on user input, the software can do one of a number of tasks from each branch in the program.

bridge tape. A magnetic tape containing data that, when loaded into an existing graphics system, alter system functionality according to unique, custom-designed specifications. Such tapes are usually employed in the interim between production releases of a graphics software system.

B-spline. Refers to a curve or curved surface constructed on a graphics system using a series of minute lines determined by geometric function calculations.

buffer. A temporary storage device used to compensate for a difference in data flow rates or in time of data flow events when transmitting data from one device to another. Buffered data are immediately available for use when needed and need not be reread from an input device.

bug. Computer slang for a programing error severe enough to render either software or hardware integrated circuits incapable of performing tasks for which they were designed.

build. 1. Refers to the process of integrating several software subsystems into one major graphics system suitable for release to customers. 2. The manufacture of hardware components in a graphics system.

button. A function switch which operates through a pressure sensitive surface.

byte. A single group of binary digits processed in parallel (as a unit). Sometimes called a "word."
Usage: Originally, a byte was always eight bits and it is still sometimes used that way. However, recent hardware is based on 16-bit, 32-bit, and 64-bit words, which are also sometimes called bytes.

C

CAD (Computer-Aided Design). Refers to the process of and methods for using computer systems as tools in the creation or modification of product-related designs. *See also* "CAD/CAM."

CAD/CAM (Computer-Aided Design/Computer-Aided Manufacturing). A general term that refers to the entire industry of computer graphics, including all aspects of computer-aided design and manufacturing, numerical control, drafting, and all other computer graphics applications.

CAD Film Plotter. A computer-aided design system that plots on-line graphic data directly onto photographic film. The D 148H CAD Film Plotter based on the PDP 11 central processing unit is manufactured by Dicomed Corporation.

CADD (Computer-Aided Design and Drafting). Refers to any computer system used in the creation and modification of product designs. Used synonymously with "computer-aided design (CAD)."

CAI (Computer-Aided Instruction). Describes any on-line training system that employs a computer to prompt and guide a student on some specified subject. Such systems are now being applied to the training of graphics system operators.

call. To transfer processing control to a specified subroutine or to a specified peripheral device or graphics workstation.

CAM (Computer-Aided Manufacturing). Refers to the process of or methods for using computer systems as tools in any or all phases of product manufacturing. *See also* "CAD/CAM."

canned cycle. A processing function or series of functions in a predetermined sequence which always conclude in the same result. A standardized process that can be called repeatedly and at any time. Used in graphics systems to produce drawings used over and over in the course of day-to-day operations.

carriage return. Very often abbreviated to CR. Refers to the key on the keyboard of workstations that concludes a line of entered data or activates the command sequence entered on the command line. This action returns the cursor to the leftmost position on the line in imitation of the carriage of a typewriter.

Cartesian coordinate system. A two- or three-dimensional system of measuring distances in which the location of a point is defined as its distance from two or three straight lines intersecting at right angles. Named after the mathematician René Descartes and used as the basis of coordinate measurements in all computer graphics systems.

cartridge disk. A disk storage device designed to be easily removed from the drive for more convenient data transfers. The cartridge usually consists of one magnetized platter rather than several as in standard disks.

CAT (Computer-Aided Testing). Refers to the use of a computer graphics system in evaluating the viability of product designs and models.

catalog. A set of descriptive items specific enough to allow on-line files to be distinguished from one another and then located in the directory structure. Used in graphics systems to organize files of part and assembly designs.

cathode-ray tube (CRT). A vacuum tube used for display of on-line graphic data. It produces a visible pattern when its electron beam is focused on a small cross section of a luminescent screen. The beam can be varied in location and intensity to display any form.

CC-80. An intelligent graphics workstation manufactured by Auto-trol Technology Corporation.

CDA (Computer Drafting Aid System). An interactive graphics system produced by Data Technology, Inc. and based on the PDP11 central processing unit.

cell matrix. A rectangular arrangement of dots from which a subset may be chosen which creates a pattern representing an alphanumeric character when output.

center of projection. The central, single point in a drawing from which all lines emanate as they simulate a three-dimensional projection.

centerline. A vector defining the precise vertical or horizontal middle on an object, file, or surface. *See also* CL tape.

central processing unit (CPU). That part of a computing system containing the circuits that control and execute all instructions that perform work on data in the system. These circuits include storage registers, arithmetic and logic units, and special register groups.

chaining. Linking a series of entities or files in a graphics data base so that an operator can search in either direction for a specific entity within the chain.

chamfer. A beveled edge produced at the intersection of two lines in a production drawing.

character. A letter, digit, or special character represented on the keyboard. When displayed, characters are drawn by an arrangement of dots or by connected straight lines.

character generator. A device which scans and chooses the appropriate character pattern from a group of permanently stored patterns and outputs the pattern at a specified position on an output device.

character recognition. Refers to the ability of an input device to recognize graphic characters automatically. Used to input textual data into an on-line file by such means as optical scanning of IBM Selectric typewriter characters.

character set. Refers to the complete group of keyboard symbols available for use in a specific computer system. The most commonly used character set is the 128-character ASCII.

character string. Any group of characters acted upon in a computer system as though they were a single unit.

check bit. A single binary digit used to determine the parity status of a byte of data. Sometimes called a ''parity bit.''

check surface. A surface set aside in an engineering or design model expressly for use as a stopping place or turning location for a tooling device or cutter.

CIM (Computer Integrated Manufacturing). A system consisting of the merger of a turnkey CAD/CAM system with the tasks of physical distribution, inventory control, cost accounting, purchasing, and others for the purpose of maintaining complete manufacturing control.

circle. A continuous plane curve that is everywhere equidistant from a fixed point called the center point. Circle creation is an automated function of virtually all computer graphics systems.

CL file. A cutter location file on a numerical control system.

CL tape (cutterline or centerline). Describes the output of a computer-written numerical control tape (paper or magnetic) on which the location of the center tool path is recorded. This tape is usually processed again before use in production processes in order to make adjustments for specific tool and specific part requirements.

clearance plane. An imaginary surface over a part surface being manufactured by a computer-aided manufacturing system above which a machine tool can move without damaging the part.

clip boundary. The physical limit in a graphics file beyond which data are either not visible or automatically deleted.

clipping. Refers to any graphic data outside a specified boundary that are removed from the display or the file. It is often used in mapping applications to remove data that would otherwise confuse the map being represented. Sometimes it also refers to graphic data that are outside the viewing area of a drawing displayed on a cathode-ray tube.

CNC. *See* computer numerical control.

coaxial cable. Round transmitting wire consisting of a central conductor, often a copper tube, surrounded by another conductor of larger diameter, often copper braid. It is used to attach peripherals to a workstation or central processing unit or to provide communications among a network of independent workstations or systems.

code. Refers to software in its written form.

color. Always used in the context of describing output. The function of color output is to be able to distinguish among the individual elements of a complex drawing. Cathode-ray tubes, plotters, and hard copy units are the most common color output devices on a graphics system.

color table. A chart illustrating the range of colors available for output display in a graphics system. Varying hues are made by mixing the primary colors in different intensity levels.

COM (Computer Output Microfilm). Refers to the conversion of on-line computer data into a form that can be written to microfilm. Both textual and graphic data can be converted in this way.

command. An instruction entered by the user which determines what graphics operation is to be executed next.

command-driven. Describes a computer graphics system that operates only when a user enters specified key words followed by qualifying parameters. Contrast with "menu-driven."

communication. The transmission of data between devices. Coaxial cable, telephone hookups, and satellites are the usual means of communication between graphics systems or between graphics systems and their peripherals.

communications network. A group of interconnected devices that can operate independently or in conjunction with one another. In computer graphics, networks are most often organized to join the power of several minicomputer-based systems into one large system capable of sharing data and peripheral devices. The communication usually occurs over coaxial cable hookups.

compile. 1. Refers to the process by which a high-level source program is transformed by another program (called the "compiler") into machine-level language that can be processed by the system hardware directly. 2. The process of gathering together in one file, data from a number of different sources.

component. 1. Any set of graphic data that can be named and stored as an independent file. 2. In geometry, it describes one of a set of two or more vectors having a sum equal to some other designated vector.

composite color. Color output from a computer graphics system described in terms of its hue and its brightness and encoded in a single video signal.

composite curve. A series of curves grouped together as a single entity so that they appear to be a single curve.

Compumill.™ A vertical, three-axis milling machine used for precision machining applications. It is manufactured by Computool Corporation.

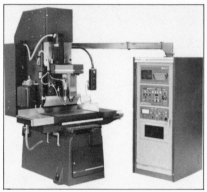

Compuscanner.™ A three-axis coordinate measuring machine manufactured by Computool Corporation to digitize graphic data.

Compuscope.™ A graphics design station manufactured by Computool Corporation for use in constructing three-dimensional drawings, editing data, and generating machine tooling programs.

Compumill.™ A computer-controlled, three-axis milling machine.

Compuscanner.™ A three-axis coordinate measuring machine.

Compuscope.™ A graphics design station.

computer-aided. Describes any task accomplished with the help of a computer. The term implies that the task was done faster than it would have been without the computer's assistance.

computer-aided design. *See* CAD.

computer-aided design and drafting. *See* CADD.

computer-aided instruction. *See* CAI.

computer-aided manufacturing. *See* CAM.

computer-aided testing. *See* CAT.

computer animation. The use of a computer graphics system to generate motion pictures.

computer-augmented. Refers to a situation wherein a computer not only aided a user in doing a task, but made the results of the work turn out better then they would have without that aid.

computer-augmented design. A computer-aided system that does more than just aid product developers in their work, but actually improves the work through automatic or suggested refinements.

Computer Drafting Aid System. *See* CDA.

computer graphics. That branch of computer science specializing in the methods of creating or modifying pictorial data, particularly in ways useful to designers, engineers, architects, and other business professionals.

Computer Integrated Manufacturing. *See* CIM.

computer network. An interconnection of two or more central processing units that can share data, memory, and peripheral devices. This kind of processing arrangement is becoming more and more common in the CAD/ CAM industry due to the diminishing cost of minicomputers and to the increasing need for data sharing among drafting, engineering, and manufacturing departments.

computer numerical control (CNC). Refers to the use of a dedicated microcomputer within a numerical control device that enables the input of data directly to the device. Very often the CNC unit is also linked directly to a central computer.

computer output microfilm. *See* COM.

concurrency. Refers to the ability of a computer system to conduct two or more tasks simultaneously. This is a valuable attribute in any graphics system running several input/output peripheral devices.

cone. A surface generated by a straight line passing through a fixed point and moving along the intersection with a fixed curve. The figure formed by such a surface.

conic generator. The part of a graphics system (including the display controller and graphics software) that draws circles or ellipses on a display surface such that the resulting figure has the illusion of three dimensions.

conic projection. A method of projecting representations of all or part of the earth's spherical surface onto a surrounding cone that is then flattened to a plane surface. This is a process commonly used in cartography and is, therefore, usually incorporated into the software of graphics system mapping applications.

console. This term is used loosely in the computer graphics industry and may refer to any one of several things: the front panel of any hardware devices where controls or indicators are located, the keyboards of a workstation which are used to communicate with the central processing unit, or the control panel for the central processing unit itself.

constraint relational. Refers to the numerically comparative attributes ''less than,'' ''greater than,'' or ''equal to.''

continuous path operation. Describes a manufacturing operation in which the movement of the machine tool is always directed by numerical controls.

contour control system. Any system which simultaneously controls the movement of two or more axes. Usually applied to numerical control systems.

contouring. Refers to the creation of the outline of a figure, body, or mass. In computer graphics, it usually describes a method of numerical control machining wherein the outlines of a part are cut by keeping the tool in constant contact with the workpiece.

Contouring System. A collection of software routines produced by Precision Visuals, Inc. that provides grid generation and contouring capabilities for creating maps on a computer graphics system.

contrast. Refers to the difference between the highest and lowest intensity levels available on a graphics display device.

control characters. Refers to keyboard characters that, when entered, are interpreted by a device as instructions for the control of that device and are not transmitted further.

controller. Any hardware or software element or group of elements through which system data are converted during input and output to a peripheral device for the purpose of effecting communications between the system and the peripheral.

coordinate. Any data value that specifies a graphics location. The values are usually determined through either a relative or absolute geometric system.

coordinate system. A set of two or three magnitudes used to determine the position of a geometric shape in two or three dimensions. All locations are then defined in terms of the origin of that coordinate system. Most computer graphics systems permit the construction of geometric shapes in three dimensions.

coordinated dimensioning. A system of determining or quantifying dimensions whereby points are defined as being a specific length and direction from a reference point that is itself positioned with respect to defined axes.

core memory. Refers to the temporary data storage within the central processing unit of a graphics system which employs a core of magnetic material surrounded by a coil of wire. The core can be magnetized with a positive or negative charge to represent the binary digits one and zero.

CPU. *See* central processing unit.

critical path method. A technique for scheduling and tracking all phases of a complex manufacturing project. Often, the computer-aided manufacturing system contains an on-line file in which this information is collected and stored.

cross hairs. Two intersecting lines, one horizontal, one vertical, on an input/output device wherein their intersection point marks the active cursor position of a graphics system.

cross section slice. The intersection of a plane with a three-dimensional graphics entity.

crosshatching. Refers to the shading of some portion of a drawing with a pattern of lines or figures repeated across the area being shaded.

CRT. *See* cathode-ray tube.

cubic spline. A spline curve derived from explicit or parametric cubic polynomial arcs. The geometry required to produce cubic splines is often a built-in function of computer-aided manufacturing software packages.

Cuechart.™ A manual of predesigned bar, pie, and line charts produced by Integrated Software Systems Corporation for use with their Tell-A-Graph software.

current. The term used to describe the state of a graphics system or system component at the present time to the exclusion of previous or future states.

cursor. A position indicator often used on a cathrode-ray tube screen to pinpoint where data will be input. The cursor is often represented by a small cross or by a blinking block of light.

cursor control keys. Refers to those keys on a workstation keyboard that control the movement of the cursor symbol on the display screen.

cut plane. A planar surface used to intersect a three-dimensional graphics entity in order to derive a cross section.

cut vector. Refers to the direction and magnitude of a single line in a cutter path.

cutter compensation. Refers to the adjustment of a cutter path required to compensate for the variance in the cutting tool radius.

cutter path. The line described by the motion of a cutting tool controlled by a computer-aided manufacturing system. Also the graphic data representing that line in a graphics file.

cutterline. A vector or series of vectors in a graphics file representing the path a cutting tool would take when manufacturing a machined part. *See* CL tape.

cycle. A time interval in which a characteristic or repeated event occurs. In a graphics system most processing is said to run in machine cycles.

cylinder slice. An ellipse determined by the intersection of a cylinder and a plane.

D

data. Information in a form suitable for processing by a computer. More generally it refers to any set of organized information.
Usage: In everyday use data can take a singular or a plural verb so long as its use is consistent within the sentence. In the technical word of computer graphics, however, data is usually plural; "datum" is the recognized singular form.

data base. An organized collection of data containing information fundamental to a business or industry or job. More generally, all the data on magnetic media available for use by a specified computer system.
Usage: In the past, data base referred to a highly organized and consistent set of data that could be accessed through a "database management system" which enabled wholesale updates, data searches, and reads without constraining access by other users. In more recent usage, the term has come to refer to any collection of data without regard to its organization. However, the distinction between these two senses of the term can be preserved, as it is in this glossary, by spelling the first closed (database) and the second open (data base).

data bus. A piece of computer hardware that transmits coded data in either parallel or series mode between processors or other hardware components in a graphics system.

data file. A set of related data in which all records are organized alike and which can be accessed under a single name.

data item. A single member of a set of data. The set may be of any data configuration including bits, bytes, files, or directories.

data processing. Refers to any sequence of machine-controlled operations which act on data to produce some predictable, desired result. Graphics systems are one kind of data processing system.

data reduction. Refers to the transformation of raw, unprocessed data into a form more useful to a graphics system. It is a process often used on computer-aided manufacturing systems to smooth design lines and reduce extraneous or inexact information.

data tablet. The generic name for a variety of data entry devices consisting of a pen or stylus and a board with a coordinate grid superimposed on its surface. When the pen touches the board, graphic information describing the location of the point in the x and y axes is transmitted to special input registers.

database. An organized collection of on-line data having a structure that enables the user to ask for and find any single item or group of data in the collection using automatic means.

database management system (DBMS). A comprehensive software system which facilitates the updating, editing, and accessing of data in a unified database operating in a multiuser environment.

Datapath.™ A magnetic tape drive manufactured by Computool Corporation for use with machine tool controllers.

Datatizer.™ A high-resolution, absolute digitizer manufactured by GTCO Corporation which is capable of digitizing through one inch of material.

DBMS. *See* database management system.

debug. The process of detecting, locating, and correcting errors in software routines.

deceleration distance. Refers to the space required for a hardware device to slow to a stop along an axis of motion in order to prevent overshooting a desired position. Often said of plotters or numerically controlled tools.

decluttering. The selective deletion of unimportant data from a complex graphics file which allows the operator to more easily see aspects of the drawing that are important.

dedicated computer. Describes a computer system committed to a single function or application; or, a computer that *can be* committed to such a singular use. Dedicated computers arose with the advent of mini- and microcomputers, whereas before, when only mainframe computers were in use, their expense required them to be used simultaneously for many functions in a time-sharing environment.

delete. To remove data from a graphics data base.

delimiter. A symbol that establishes boundaries between items of data or between elements of a command on the command line. Graphic commands often have many options; these must be separated by delimiters before they can be interpreted correctly by the system.

depth. The dimension or size of the z coordinate.

depth control. The ability to alter the extent of the z axis or the extent of a graphics entity in the z axis.

depth cueing. A display system feature that simulates three dimensions by shading or by displaying certain vectors at different intensities.

design language. Refers to a special category of programing languages in which the statements and syntax were designed for use in a specific design discipline.

detail. Any small section of a larger graphics entity or file.

developable surface layout. A graphics file consisting of the translation of a three-dimensional object into a two-dimensional surface by unrolling and flattening the object.

device. A general term used to describe any mechanical, electrical, or electronic apparatus that may be a part of a graphics system.

device independent. Describes a computer program that can control any of a group of similar hardware devices, e.g., a variety of line printers.

diagnostic. Refers to the process, methods, or tools applied to the detection and isolation of malfunctions and errors in the components of a computing system.

diagnostic routine. A specially designed software program that locates and identifies errors in a specific component of a computing system.

Digipad.ⓉⓂ A family of electromagnetic digitizers manufactured by GTCO Corporation.

digit. The Arabic numerals 0–9 that represent the integers in the base ten numbering system. In the binary system of numbering used by computer systems the digits 0 and 1 are used.

digital. Refers to data represented in the form of digits. In a computer system based on the binary system, the digits are either one or zero.

digital computer. A computer that performs all operations with quantities represented as digits. Nearly all computer systems use the binary system and, therefore, employ only the digits one and zero. Most graphics systems are based on digital computers. Differs from the analog computer wherein fluctuating signal strengths represent data in continuous form.

digitize. Refers to the use of digits to represent graphic data wherein a physical quantity is transformed into a digital representation of the quantity.

digitizer. A peripheral device often associated with computer graphics systems that converts graphic figures into digital form. In a typical application a drawing is placed on the surface of the device and is traced by the operator with a cursor or stylus. The traced form is then converted to digital data that can be processed by the central processing unit.

digitizing. Refers to the process of converting graphic representations into digital data that can be processed by a computer graphics system.

dimension. 1. *Noun*: any measure of spatial extent, expecially the height, width, and depth of objects. 2. *Verb*: refers to the creation or determination of spatial extent for a given object.

disable. A command which prevents further operation of a peripheral device.

disabled. Describes the condition of a system component that has, for any reason, quit functioning.

disk. A data storage device consisting of one or more flat circular plates coated with magnetized material. Data are read or written on the disk with read/write heads that skim the surface of the disk as it spins at high speed on a central spindle.

disk operating system (DOS). A computer system in which programs and data use disk memory rather than core memory as the main operating feature.

disk partition. A logical portion of a disk that provides an organization allowing smaller blocks of data to be handled more conveniently.

dispatching. Refers to the selection and sequencing of processing tasks and the assignment of those tasks to users and to workstations. Dispatching is sometimes done by the system manager and is sometimes handled automatically by a software dispatcher.

display. Refers to the process of creating a visual representative of graphic data on an output device (usually a cathode-ray tube) or to the image being represented.

display background. Refers to the part of displayed graphic data that is not part of the image being processed. The background display cannot be altered by the user, but is intended to highlight or define that part of the display that can be altered.

display character generator. That part of a graphics system designed to produce alphanumeric characters from a predefined set of symbols and geometric entities. These characters are then displayed on a graphics output device.

display console. An input/output device consisting of a display screen and an input keyboard. Also known as a workstation.

display cycle. Refers to the time it takes a display screen to be completely refreshed.

display device. Any output device capable of producing a visual representation of graphic data. The most common display devices are cathode-ray tube screens, plotters, and hard copy units. Usually, however, the term refers to cathode-ray tube screens.

display foreground. Refers to the graphic data being displayed on a cathode-ray tube that are subject to alteration by the user.

display image. That portion of a displayed graphics file that is currently visible on the display device.

display list. Any listing of on-line information output on a display device. Usually, however, it refers to a menu displayed on an interactive graphics system.

display menu. A list of choices displayed on a graphics output device from which the user can choose the next function to be executed.

display surface. Refers to the medium upon which a visual representation of graphic data is made, e.g., plotter paper, cathode-ray tube screen, film, etc.

display terminal. An input/output device with a cathode-ray tube and keyboard that can be used to enter or view graphic data on a graphics system.

display tolerance. Refers to the measure of accuracy with which graphic data can be output.

Disspla.™ A library of high-level graphic art quality, general-purpose line, bar, and pie charts, three-dimensional surface charts, maps, and contours produced by Integrated Software Systems Corporation.

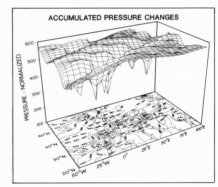

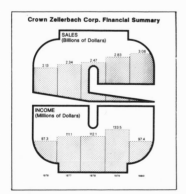

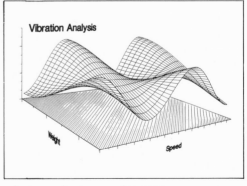

Disspla.™ A library of general purpose charts, graphs, maps, and contours.

distributed computer network. A group of separate but associated computer systems that can communicate with one another and share data.

distributed numerical control. *See* DNC.

distributed plotting system. A system that transmits plot data to multiple drafting systems. Such systems can be stand-alone or part of a larger, distributed plotter network.

Distributed Plotting System. Transmits plot data to multiple drafting systems.

distributed processing. Refers to the processing of data in a distributed computer network environment. This kind of processing permits data sharing and peripheral sharing by a group of separate computers with the effect of making more efficient use of resources than is usually possible in centralized processing.

DI-3000.℠ An integrated system of graphics software tools, consisting of 160 user-callable subroutines, developed by Precision Visuals, Inc.

DNC (Distributed Numerical Control). Refers to any numerical control system that utilizes more than one graphics workstation.

documentation. Refers to all manner of printed or on-line textual material used for reference purposes by operators of graphics systems.

DOS. *See* disk operating system.

dot matrix. A pattern of dots on a two-dimensional coordinate system or two-dimensional array.

dot matrix printer. An output device that represents graphic data by marking individual dots on a two-dimensional coordinate system.

double buffering. A method for increasing processing speed in a graphics system by which two data buffers are addressed alternately; while the first buffer is transmitting data, the second is ready to receive data.

double precision. Refers to the use of two bytes rather than one byte to represent a number. This technique increases the accuracy of calculations often required for manufacturing and design applications.

downloading. A process of loading data from one location to another so that processing can begin. It often applies to loading software from a central processing unit to an intelligent terminal.

downtime. Refers to the time interval during which a device or system is inoperable due to a failure.

drawing. Refers to the process of creating a line with a computer graphics system in which a vector is generated from the current position to a second coordinate location that in turn becomes the current position after the vector is generated.

drill tape. A tape punched with numerical control commands and used to operate automatic hole drilling equipment.

driver. Refers to the programs that control the operation of peripheral devices and which are the interfaces between the device and the central processing unit.

drum plotter. A special kind of plotter that produces drawings on media fixed to a rotating cylinder. The plotting head moves along one axis of the drawing while the cylinder rotates to provide movement for the other axis. Curves are plotted by moving the head and the drum simultaneously.

dumb terminal. A computer terminal used to call data for viewing but from which no processing can be done.

dump. Refers to the process of copying the contents of one section of memory to another.

dynamic display. Any visual representation of graphic data in which the data appear to move or change over time. The movement may be due to the change in position of the data on the device or due to a series of graphic entities being displayed in succession.

dynamic dump. Refers to a storage dump that is performed during the execution of a program.

dynamic refresh. Allows the display of whole figures wherein the data are not actually entered into the drawing but are held in a temporary buffer. In this way, users can see how the data fit the drawing before entering the items permanently into the data base. Dynamic refresh figures are usually displayed with a different intensity or color than is used to display the data already in the drawing.

dynamic storage. A method of storing data in which it must be periodically refreshed to remain valid.

E

EBCDIC (Extended Binary Coded Decimal Interchange Code). An 8-bit code used to represent 256 numbers, letters, and characters in a computer system. This code was developed by IBM and is used primarily by IBM equipment.

echo check. Refers to a method of checking the validity of transmitted data in which the data received are sent back to the sending device for comparison with the original data.

edit. Refers to the process of rearranging or modifying on-line data. In computer graphics, editing consists primarily of modifying the graphic data of drawings and figures.

editor. A software application which allows a user to perform editing operations on computer data. Some editors are designed for specific editing functions, e.g., editing text, graphics, or program statements.

EDP. *See* electronic data processing.

effective speed. Refers to the operating speed of computer system components at which the equipment can operate most efficiently given the slowing effects of user interaction, data transmission and access, and any other operations required to run the equipment. Effective speed is almost always less than rated speed.

ELD (Electrical Ladder Diagramer). An applications package for producing electrical control diagrams manufactured by Gerber Systems Technology, Inc.

Electrical Ladder Diagramer. *See* ELD.

electronic data processing (EDP). A very general term referring to any data manipulation conducted with the aid of a computer.

electrostatic plotter. An output device that draws graphic data on paper using static electrical energy to determine vectors.

element. Refers either to a single item of data or to a single, specified portion of a graphic data file.

ellipse. A plane curve in the shape of an oval wherein the figure can be divided into four equal parts. Ellipse creation is an automated function of virtually all computer graphics systems.

emulate. A method of data processing by which one component of a graphics system imitates another for the purpose of achieving the same results that would derive from using the component being imitated.

emulation. 1. Refers to the imitation of a computing function by a system not originally designed to perform that function. 2. The use of hardware or software to execute programs written for use on another system.

emulator. A hardware or software component of a computer system that emulates.

enable. Refers to the restoration of function to a system component that was suppressed or shut down.

end point. 1. The terminal points of a line or the coordinates of those points. 2. The logical conclusion of a processing operation.

end-of-file mark (EOF). A single, specific code attached to the end of a file that indicates, during read operations, that the end of the file has been reached.

end-of-tape marker. A physical mark placed on a magnetic tape to indicate the boundaries of the area on which recorded data may be written.

engineering simulation. A set of programs that run on a graphics system which are designed to permit testing of engineering algorithms and designs under conditions representative of real conditions.

entity. A collection of data that has an independent and distinct existence within a graphics file or data base.

entity sequence. The chronological order in which a series of entities has been created.

EOF. *See* end-of-file mark.

ergonomics. The study of the physical relationship between people and their work environment. The term is often applied more specifically to the study of fitting production equipment to the physical and behavioral characteristics of workers. Such studies are often applied to the design of graphics workstations.

EXAPT. Refers to an extended subset of the computer-aided manufacturing language APT. EXAPT processors are most commonly used in point-to-point manufacturing tools and for lathe work.

execution. Refers to the processing of an instruction or to the performance of a routine on a computer system.

exploded view. An illustration, photograph, or diagram of a solid construction showing its parts separately, but in positions which indicate their relationships to the whole. Often used when plotting or displaying on-line graphic data.

Extended Binary Coded Decimal Interchange Code. *See* EBCDIC.

extended geometry. Geometric constructions which have two or three dimensions.

extensible language processor. A software routine that allows users to define and implement new features into an existing computer language. By means of various definitions facilities, a base language can be extended to include new data structures, operations, and notations.

extrema. Points in a file or graphics entity located the greatest distance apart in each axis and which thereby establish the extreme dimensions of that file or entity.

F

fabrication. 1. Refers to the processing of manufacturing materials to desired specifications. 2. Also refers to the object resulting from a computer-aided manufacturing process.

feed rate. An expression used to quantify the speed of movement of a component of a CAD/CAM system. This movement could be related to paper or magnetic tape, a machining tool, cutting device, or disk spindle rotation.

FEM. *See* finite element modeling.

file. Any collection of logically related data. These data may then be stored or processed as a single unit.

file maintenance. Refers to any of the activities of keeping data files current, such as adding, altering, or deleting parts of those files, so that they always reflect accurate, up-to-date information.

file protection. Refers to the methods of preventing unauthorized users from tampering with data in certain files.

fill. To put graphic data, such as crosshatching or shading, into an empty but defined area within a graphics file.

fillet. An arc tangentially connecting two curves, lines, or points.

finite element modeling (FEM). A standard applications package on computer-aided manufacturing systems which allows the operator to build a construction part and then divide that part into discrete elements each of which can be analyzed and tested.

fitting. Refers to the calculation of a curve, surface, or line that fits most accurately to a set of data points and design criteria. This technique can be employed automatically with most computer graphics systems.

fixed point. A method of representing numerical values in a computer graphics system wherein the numbers are shown with the decimal point in a single, stationary position. Contrast with ''floating-point representation.''

fixed sequential format. A format for creating numerical control tapes wherein each word in the format is identified by its position relative to all other words.

fixed word length. Describes a computer system wherein data are treated in units (words) of a specific and unalterable number of bits. All words (bytes) in the system are, therefore, the same length.

flag. Any hardware or software indicator used to identify a byte, file, or component of a graphics system.

flatbed plotter. Any graphics output plotter that produces images on any medium mounted on a horizontal table.

flicker. The visible flashing of the display on a cathode-ray tube that occurs when the refresh speed is not fast enough to compensate for natural luminance decay on the screen.

floating-point representation. A method of storing numbers in a computer where the location of the decimal point is determined by multiplying a stored exponent times a fixed positive integer base. This process allows very large and very small numbers to be stored more efficiently and without rounding. This results in more accurate calculations such as those often required in CAD/CAM operations restricted by very close tolerances.

floating zero. Applies to a numerical control system in which the point of reference may be set at any position over the area covered by the machine tool.

floppy disk. A magnetic data recording device consisting of a flexible platter rotating around a central spindle.

flow chart. A schematic representation of a sequence of operations that illustrate analyses, problem solutions, data flow, and the like. Often standards symbols are used to depict decisions, alternatives, and end points.

flow line. In a flow chart, the line representing the logical connection between the flow chart symbols.

flow sheet. Synonomous with "flow chart." Sometimes used to organize procedures required by CAD/CAM operations.

flowcharter. A computer program that generates flow charts automatically on a graphics system.

font. A complete set of graphic symbols, including all the alphanumeric characters, of one size and face. Most computer graphics systems have many on-line fonts available for use.

foreground processing. Refers to data processing tasks which are of high priority. These tasks, often the result of real-time entries, take precedence, through the use of interrupts, over all background processes.

format. Refers to the specific physical arrangement of data. Formats may dictate both how data are stored and displayed.

formatted display. The displayed output of graphic data in which the attributes or contents of one or more display fields have been defined by the user.

formula translation. *See* FORTRAN.

FORTRAN (FORmula TRANslation). A high-level programming language designed specifically for applications in the physical sciences. FORTRAN is very commonly used to write CAD/CAM applications.

4-D digitizer. A tablet digitizer manufactured by GTCO Corporation which can output the magnitude and direction of the stylus tilt as well as three-dimensional digital information.

full frame. Refers to the process by which a display image is scaled to use the entire viewing area of a display device.

function. Any processing task done on a computer graphics system that has been automated and executes simply by pressing a key or entering a command.

function keypad. An input device consisting of a group of function keys.

function keys. Refers to the input keys on data entry devices which, when pressed, initiate a particular graphics operation on a computer graphics system. In this way users can, with a single keystroke, activate functions that might otherwise require a long series of keystrokes to initiate.

G

garbage. Refers to inaccurate, extraneous, or indecipherable data generated by a computer graphics system.

gateway. Refers to a data communications pathway in a distributed graphics system. More specifically, it usually refers to a node in a distributed processing network that can communicate with a minicomputer or mainframe outside the network.

general processor. Refers to the software that drives numerical control programs.

generation. Refers to the process by which the user of a computer graphics system inputs various parameters and definitions to a software routine that uses the information to produce another program or a graphic entity automatically.

geometry. 1. That branch of mathematics pertaining to the study of the properties of points, lines, angles, surfaces, and solids. 2. Refers to the specific physical arrangement of lines that make up the shape of a specific physical or graphics entity.

G-Pack. A technical publication configuration package produced by Information Displays, Inc. and consisting of the Composition Processor, the Production Editing Workstation, and the digital phototypesetter or laser printer interface.

Grafmaker.™ An integrated system of graphic software tools developed by Precision Visuals, Inc. for designing and viewing line graphs, bar graphs, and pie charts.

Grafmaster.™ A panel-driven system which provides standard interface panels for interactively generating both simple and complex charts—including line graphs, pie charts, bar graphs, word charts, and combinations thereof—on a broad range of graphic display devices. The system is manufactured by Precision Visuals, Inc.

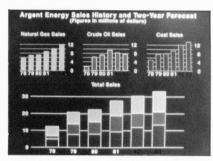

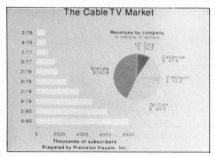

Grafmaster.™ Can be used to generate a variety of charts and graphs.

graphics. 1. The creation of drawings in accordance with the axioms of mathematics. 2. The calculation, through established mathematical procedures, of physical forces, stresses, strengths, etc. from such drawings. *Usage:* Although plural, the word is commonly used with a singular verb.

graphics display. Describes any graphics data output device that can present an image of graphic data derived from a computer graphics system.

graphics input device. Any hardware component of a graphics system that enables the user to enter graphic data.

Graphics Processing Language. *See* GRAPL.

graphics tablet. A graphics input device consisting of a flat surface on which points can be identified with a stylus, light pen, or cursor.

Graphover.™ A graphics system manufactured by New Media Graphics Corporation that generates a graphics overlay which is then superimposed in perfect synchronization on top of a video picture from videotape, videodisc, or television camera.

GRAPL (GRAphics Processing Language). Pronounced "grapple." A high-level programing language used primarily in computer-aided manufacturing systems.

gray scale. Refers to the level of brightness that describes the illumination of a cathode-ray tube screen.

grid. Any pattern of horizontal and vertical lines that form squares of uniform size over a surface. In computer graphics, grids form the basis by which point positions are defined.

grid roundoff. A method of digitizing in which entered points are automatically moved to the nearest intersection of grid lines so that the distance between points will have a base of uniformity.

GS-32. A menu-driven graphics software system manufactured by Autotrol Technology Corporation. The system is used primarily for mechanical design and manufacturing applications.

GS-1000. A design and drafting graphics software system manufactured by Auto-trol Technology Corporation.

H

handshaking. Refers to the exchange of predetermined signals between hardware devices to determine whether they can accurately transfer data between them.

hard copy. A printed copy of graphic data produced on or stored by a computer graphics system.

hard copy unit. A peripheral device associated with a computer graphics system that produces printed copies of on-line graphic data. Usually refers more specifically to small, tabletop copy units rather than large, free-standing plotters or printers.

hardware. The physical devices composing a computer graphics system, including all mechanical, magnetic, and electronic components.

hardwired. Refers to those functions of a computer graphics system that are determined by the hardware configuration, including instructions contained in integrated circuit chips, cables, wires, and other electrical connectors.

hatching. Refers to the process of filling a specified area within a graphics file with a pattern of parallel lines.

hidden line removal. Refers to the processes of deleting line segments from a drawing when they would be obscured were the object displayed as a solid three-dimensional figure. Many computer graphics systems can remove such hidden lines automatically.

hidden lines. Refers to the line segments of a graphics entity that would be obscured from view were the object displayed as a solid three-dimensional figure.

hidden objects. Refers to distinct graphic entities that would be obscured from view by other entities were they displayed as solids.

hidden surface. Refers to entire surfaces or planes that would be obscured from view were the graphics figure displayed as a three-dimensional solid.

high level language. Refers to any programing language used to write application software packages. FORTRAN is an example of such a language that is commonly used to write graphics software.

Hip1Øt.™ A low-cost, high-quality micrographic plotter available with an array of standard and optional features. Hip1Øt plotters are manufactured by Houston Instrument, a division of Bausch and Lomb.

Hip1Øt.™ A standard computer graphics ink plotter.

host computer. The central processing unit which provides processing support to other processors, workstations, or peripheral devices. The devices being supported usually cannot function on their own, whereas the host can and does operate independently.

human factors engineering. Much in vogue in the design of graphics systems, this phrase describes attempts to adapt hardware to a shape that is conducive to use by people. The phrase is awkward because it is intended to imply that both physical and psychological requirements of users have been accounted for in the design process.

hyperbola. A graphics entity consisting of a curve formed by the intersection of a cone and a plane inclined more steeply to the base than to the side of the cone.

I

ICAPS™ (Integrated Composition And Production Software). A composition and production software system produced by Information Displays, Inc. that conducts automatic photocomposition and make-up for technical publications. The system merges and formats illustrations, tables, graphs, text, page numbers, headers, footers, etc.

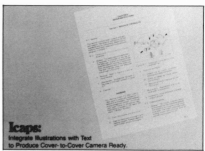

ICAPS.™ Integrates illustrations with text to produce cover-to-cover camera ready copy.

ID (Intelligent Digitizer). The name given to all models of a line of digitizers manufactured by Summagraphics Corporation which features a variety of sizes, interfaces, and accessories.

IDRAW.™ An interactive graphics software package designed by Information Displays, Inc. for use on its line of turnkey computer graphics systems.

IDS-80. The name of a turnkey, multistation CAD/CAM system manufactured by Gerber Systems Technology, Inc.

IDRAW.™ Interactively create, manipulate, and manage technical illustrations.

IDS-80. A CAD/CAM system from Gerber Systems Technology, Inc.

IGES (Initial Graphics Exchange Specification). A program focusing the efforts of all major computer graphics vendors on the development and documentation of industry standards enabling the exchange of graphic data among those vendors and their customers. The group founds its work on the premise that as computer graphics systems become more prevalent, the ability to fully use this equipment depends more and more on the ability to communicate among systems.

image. In computer graphics, refers to the output form of on-line graphics data, i.e., a displayed or drawn representation of a graphics file.

image enhancement. Any accentuation of all or part of a graphics file through such techniques as highlighting, zooming, blinking, or coloring.

image processing. To input graphic data into a computer graphics system, store it, and output it to a display device.

increment. Refers to the distance between any two adjacent addressable points on a graphics input/output device. This distance might well be determined by a grid superimposed on display device or by the size of a raster unit on a raster cathode-ray tube screen.

incremental coordinates. Refers to coordinate positions that are defined on the basis of their distance relative to previously defined coordinates. Sometimes referred to as relative coordinates.

incremental data. Refers to any data values—graphic or numeric—that are determined from previously defined values rather than from any absolute values.

incremental plotter. A plotting device that outputs graphic data in discrete movements of the plotting head.

incremental points. Points located equidistantly along a curve or line.

incremental system. A computer graphics system in which all data values are defined by their relative relation to a previous value rather than by their relation to some set of absolute values.

incremental vector. The distance and magnitude of a line as determined by endpoints that are relative to previously entered graphic values. Sometimes called relative vector.

index. Any guide or aid which facilitates reference. In computer graphics systems, an on-line alphabetized list of data files, directories, or graphic entities.

Infograf.™ An interactive graphics software package manufactured by Graphics Concepts, Inc. which is used for the creation of business graphs and charts.

Infograf.™ An interactive software package for the creation of business graphs.

Initial Graphics Exchange Specification. *See* IGES.

initialize. Refers to the process of setting a device or system to a predetermined starting position or state so that data processing functions can proceed from their beginning points and in their entirety.

ink jet plotter. An output device that plots by spraying a thin stream of ink onto the plotting medium rather than by touching a pen to the plotting surface.

input. Refers to the data or the process by which data are introduced into a computer graphics system.

input/output (I/O). A term used to describe the devices, processes, or data involved in communicating with a central processing unit.

inquiry. Refers to any request made by a program or system user for data stored on-line in a computer system.

instruction. A single, defined processing task such as is identified by a single programing statement.

instruction set. The entire group of processing tasks which can be performed by a specified computing system.

Integrated Composition and Production Software. *See* ICAPS.™

intelligence. The processing power resulting from the specific hardware and software configuration of a computer graphics system.

intelligent digitizer. *See* ID.

intelligent terminal. An input/output device with hardware which enables it to conduct processing functions independent of the central processing unit with which it is associated. The term is often misunderstood to mean the terminal is totally independent of a host. In fact, an intelligent terminal still requires a host processor for support.

intensity. Describes the level of brightness emitted by a cathode-ray tube. Many graphics workstations have a cathode-ray tube on which the intensity can be controlled by manipulating a switch.

interactive graphics system. A computer graphics system that requests and accepts input from an operator and allows the operator to direct the processing operations according to the requirements of a specific graphics task.

interactivity. A data processing context in which the computer system and the user work together to solve problems. Usually the interactivity consists of the software prompting the user for information which is then processed in a predetermined way. Virtually all computer graphics systems are interactive.

interface. The boundary at which two components of a computer system meet. The term may also be used to describe the communication between a user and an interactive computer system.
Usage: The term should not be applied to communications between people or groups of people.

interpolation. The determination of a value that lies between two known values through mathematical calculation. In computer graphics this process is often applied to creating curves by joining a series of straight line segments or to defining smoothing curves between specified points.

interpolator. A software application that calculates graphic interpolations by mathematical means. It is often used to define the paths of numerically controlled machining tools.

interrupt. 1. Refers to the regular, momentary hesitations built into a processing task which permit the system to test for various conditions required for the successful completion of the process. 2. To halt a processing task in such a way that it cannot be resumed automatically but requires operator intervention for resumption.

interrupt handler. A control program which preserves the interrupted program's status and register values so that processing may continue normally after the interrupting processes are complete.

I/O. *See* input/output.

Io$handler. A terminal-independent device driver manufactured by Graphics Concepts, Inc., for use on computer graphics systems.

I-Pack. A technical publishing configuration package produced by Information Displays, Inc. and consisting of their Integrated Composition and Production Software (ICAPS), the Production Editing Workstation, and the digital phototypesetter or laser printer interface.

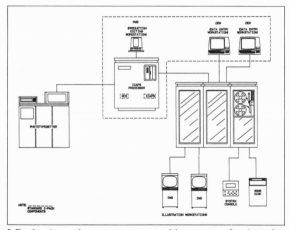

I-Pack. A turnkey computer graphics system for the publishing industry.

IS Pipeline. An intelligent printing buffer manufactured by Interactive Structures, Inc. which allows users to store sentences, paragraphs, or graphic data in random fashion prior to composing the finished document.

iterate. The repetitive performance of a processing task.

J

joystick. An upright stick attached to a data entry device that allows the user to enter coordinate values using two or three axes. The x- and y-axis values are determined by moving the stick left and right or up and back, while the z axis is controlled by twisting the stick. Very often the stick controls the position of a cursor displayed on a cathode-ray tube screen.

justify. Refers to the length, spacing, and alignment of data in a graphics system. Usually it refers specifically to textual data and to whether the text is aligned with the left, right, or both margins.

K

kernel. Describes a subset of software routines from a graphics software package.

key. Part of a record, word, or set of data that identifies or controls its use.

keyboard. A data entry device consisting of a set of buttons, each of which, when activated, tells the computer to perform some processing task. A computer graphics system keyboard usually contains alphanumeric keys, cursor control keys, function keys, and keys for various special symbols.

keystroke macro. A term developed by Gerber Systems Technology, Inc. which describes the process by which a number of processing functions are strung together and then accessed as a unit by pressing a single keyboard function key.

keyword. A word which, when entered into a computer graphics system, is interpreted to refer to a specific programed function. A keyword is called a "command" in some systems. Often the operation conducted by the identified program can be controlled or modified by entering delimiters or modifiers after the keyword on the command line.

L

label. Textual data associated logically or physically with graphic data.

laser plotter. A graphics output device that produces images on plotting media with a small laser beam.

layer. A subset of the data in a graphics file given a logical association.

layering. A logical concept that associates subgroups of graphic data within a single drawing. It allows the operator to view only those parts of a drawing being worked on and reduces the confusion that might result from viewing all parts of a very cluttered or complex file. Layers are often thought of as a series of transparencies that may be laid on top of one another in any order.

layout. The arrangement, plan, or design of something that has several parts. The graphical representation of that arrangement. Many computer graphics systems are purchased expressly to do scaled layouts of buildings, pipelines, factories, work facilities, production plants, etc.

leading zero. The zero or series of zeros that appear to the left of a number for the purpose of filling out a data field or for fixing the position of a decimal point.

library. An organized collection of related data files on any medium. Sometimes called a directory.

library routine. A standardized, debugged program maintained on a graphics system for day-to-day use by all system operators. Very often such programs are kept together in one program library.

light pen. A data entry device in the shape of a pen or wand which uses an optional lens or sensing device to record data on a graphics system. These devices are most often used on a graphics system to enter coordinate information or to select from menus.

line balancing. A management technique used in production environments wherein tasks are assigned to graphics system workstations in equal proportions, thus raising efficiency.

line feed. An operation, usually effected by a control character, that results in the next data output position being a new line on the print or display device.

line generator. Refers to a hardware or software device which produces lines on a graphics system in random configurations. Such devices are sometimes useful in various CAD/CAM software applications packages.

line segment. A portion of a longer line defined by its two end points.

line speed. Refers to the rate at which data are transmitted from one device to another. This rate is usually measured in baud, which is bits per second. A common baud rate for transmitting data on graphics systems is 9600.

line style. Refers to the method of representing a line in a graphics system, such as with dots, dashes, solid lines, or some combination thereof.

line width. The actual, physical thickness of a line in a graphics system.

linear interpolation. A method of producing lines, primarily for use on numerically controlled machines, by which they are defined according to the position of two end points rather than by their direction and magnitude.

link. Refers to any communications path between devices in a graphics system. The link may be between peripheral devices and the central processing unit, between intelligent workstations and a host, or between nodes on a distributed network. The link may consist of any kind of communication circuit, e.g., cable, modem, microwave, etc.

linkage. Refers to the process by which separate software routines are connected in a single load module that can be executed as though it were a single routine. The program that produces such load modules for use on a graphics system is usually called a linkage editor.

listing. Describes any line printer printout, but especially those that consist of programing code.

load. The process of reading data into the working registers of a computer system. This is usually done as a prelude to program execution.

load leveling. Sharing resources in the most efficient manner possible given the amount and type of work, and the equipment available on the system. One method of load leveling is distributed processing, which is used to distribute work evenly throughout a graphics system.

load module. A program or group of programs in a format suitable for immediate execution.

local node. A node within a distributed network that can communicate only with other nodes also within that network.

location. Any place in a computer graphics system in which data may be stored either permanently or temporarily.

locator device. A graphics input device used to specify coordinate data.

lock height. Refers to the maximum distance at which a cursor or stylus may be used above the surface of a digitizer tablet.

logic. Any precise system of reasoning. In computer graphics it refers to the relationship of each element of a task, device, program, or system to the whole task, device, program, or system.

logic diagram. A graphical representation of the elements and their relations in a program, task, device, or system. Most often these diagrams are used to illustrate the design of integrated circuits in the central processing unit of a graphics system.

logic element. A graphics entity that has symbolic value when used in a graphics file.

logoff. The procedure by which an authorized user concludes a working session on a specific graphics workstation. It usually results in the termination of all programs running at that station.
Usage: When used as a verb, it is spelled as two words, e.g., "logging off."

logon. The procedure by which an authorized user begins a working session on a specific graphics workstation.
Usage: When used as a verb, it is spelled as two words, i.e., ''logged on.''

loop. A sequence of software instructions that is repeated until some specified terminal condition is met or until the sequence is manually aborted.

luminance decay. Refers to the reduction in screen brightness on a cathode-ray tube that inevitably occurs over time. Many vector cathode-ray tubes automatically reduce screen brightness when a single image is displayed continually for a specified length of time; this reduces the danger of burning vectors permanently onto the screen surface.

M

machine code. 1. A system of symbolic characters that correspond to machine tool functions or characteristics. 2. Assembly language programming code.

machine control unit. A computer-aided manufacturing system designed specifically for processing and implementing numerical control programs.

machine dependent. Describes a computer program that can operate on any of a family of central processing units without requiring any alteration of the software but which cannot run on processors outside that family.

machine independent. Describes software routines that can be transported from one computer to another and then used without alteration. Programs designed for use on more than one processor.

machine instruction. A binary-coded instruction that can be recognized and executed by hardware directly, requiring no intervening processing steps.

machine language. A set of machine instructions.

machine time. The total amount of time a device is in operating condition, including both operating and idle time. Sometimes called ''up time.''

machine tool. A piece of manufacturing equipment used to form a part and which can be controlled by a graphics system with numerical control capabilities.

machineability. Refers to whether a certain manufacturing material can be shaped by machine tools controlled by a numerical control system.

macro instruction. 1. A high-level programing statement which is roughly equivalent to a series of statements in a low-level language. 2. A name given to a series of instructions and by which the series may be identified or called.

magnetic tape. A ribbon of recording material coated with a magnetic film on which data can be written. It is the most commonly used storage medium for graphic data.

main memory. Refers to the hardware data storage registers of a computer which can be accessed directly by the operating system or executing program.

mainframe. A general term describing any large and expensive central processing unit. Relatively smaller central processing units are called minicomputers.

maintenance release. A revision of an existing graphics system component that includes fixes or enhancements to that component. Contrast with ''production release.''

mapping. 1. Any process by which a graphics system translates graphic data from one coordinate system into a form useful on another coordinate system. 2. Describes a graphics software application package used in cartography.

mass properties. The physical characteristics of an object which may be considered and processed by the operator of a computer-aided manufacturing system as the object is designed.

mass storage. A magnetic storage device or medium that can hold large amounts of data, such as a large disk or magnetic tape.

master file. A permanent data file, often read and write protected, that contains authoritative information regarding some system function.

master workstation. Refers to the system workstation from which an operator can conduct system processing functions as opposed to other workstations from which only graphic functions can be conducted. Sometimes called the master console.

mathematical model. Any representation in purely mathematical form of a manufacturing workpiece. Commonly used in computer-aided manufacturing systems to aid in the design and testing of parts and assemblies.

matrix. 1. A rectangular array or two-dimensional coordinate system. 2. A logical network of input and output leads in a computer's main memory hardware.

medium. The physical material through which data are transmitted and stored, including magnetic tape, disk, paper tape, diskette, etc.

menu. A list of alternative processing functions displayed on the cathode-ray tube screen of a workstation from which the user can designate one. Many graphics systems are entirely menu-driven.

menu-driven. Describes a computer graphics system that operates when a user selects an option from a set of options displayed on the workstation screen. Contrast with "command-driven."

merge. The blending together of data from two or more different files into a new file.

message. Any collection of data with a specified meaning which can be transmitted to and from components in a graphics system or to and from systems in a network. Usually it refers more specifically to textual information that appraises the user of an internal system condition.

Metafile System. A stand-alone interactive program that gives graphics system operators the ability to determine where, when, and how to generate and display graphs and graphic images produced with other products manufactured by Precision Visuals, Inc.

microcomputer. A very small computer using only a single integrated circuit as its central processing unit. Some portions of graphics systems are driven by microcomputers.

micrographics. The processing of graphic data in a form too small to be read by the unaided human eye. Microfilm and microfiche are traditional micrographic forms.

microprocessor. A single integrated circuit chip containing a very limited instruction set. They are used to provide limited intelligence to graphics workstations and other devices.

mirroring. Refers to the display or creation of graphic data that portrays an image in exactly the reverse orientation it originally had. It is a useful technique in the design and drafting of symmetrical objects.

mnemonic. Describes any symbol chosen to aid the user in remembering. Such symbols are often used to designate graphics system commands.

model. An accurate and complete graphical representation of a real object generated by a computer graphics system.

modeling. Refers to the representation of depth, solidity, or texture in images generated by a graphics system.

MODEM (Modulator-Demodulator). A device that permits communication between two processing systems over large distances by using existing telephone lines.

modify. Refers to the process of altering, adding, or deleting data in a graphics file.

modular programing. A technique for writing software routines whereby the programing task is reduced to a series of smaller tasks which are addressed in separate routines. In this way programs can be more easily debugged and maintained by people other than the original programers. Sometimes called "structured programing."

modulator—demodulator. *See* MODEM.

module. A software program or series of programs that addresses a single programing task and can be referred to by a single name for purposes of compiling or loading.

monitor. Any hardware or software component of a graphics system that permits a user to observe and supervise some aspect of system operations.

mouse. A data entry device consisting of a small control box, often on wheels, that is pushed along a surface and transmits graphic data according to its changing position. Often function keys are mounted on the device and can be used to enter special information.

move. To change the current position on a computer graphics coordinate system.

multiplexer. A hardware device that permits a graphics system to accommodate several signals transmitted over a single channel. They are often required for distributed processing functions.

multiprocessing. Refers to the simultaneous execution of two or more programs by a single computer graphics system. Most systems now have this capability.

multitasking. The simultaneous execution of two or more programing functions by an operating system.

N

name. To associate a specified label with a graphics symbol, entity, file, or directory that can be used to address that object.

National Computer Graphics Association. *See* NCGA.

NC. *See* numerical control.

NCGA (National Computer Graphics Association). A professional society, with headquarters in Arlington, Virginia, consisting of academics, businessmen and women, and consultants interested in the computer graphics industry.

nesting. 1. Refers to establishing a hierarchy of priorities in a system of hardware or software components so that processing conflicts are avoided. 2. Refers to the placement of a set of programed instructions within a larger set. 3. In manufacturing processes, refers to the arrangement of part patterns on metal sheets or other manufacturing material so that waste of the material is held to a minimum. Many computer-aided manufacturing systems can do such nesting automatically.

net. A group of interconnected pins through which electric signals are sent and received in the hardware components of a computer graphics system.

netlist. A file containing the names, symbols, and connection point coordinates which make up a net.

networking. Refers to a special kind of system configuration in which two or more central processors are linked enabling them to share work loads and data bases. Each processor participating in such a network is called a node. Sometimes called distributed processing.

node. An individual processor which is part of a processing network.

normal axis. The third, unobservable axis of a three-dimensional object being displayed in only two dimensions.

notation. Any defined, symbolic system for representing data.

number spaces. Refers to the entire addressable area available in a specified Cartesian coordinate system. This space may exceed the area being displayed on a workstation or digitizer and may, depending on the graphics system, actually be infinite.

numerical analysis. Refers to the use of mathematics to define, design, or test geometric quantities used in CAD/CAM installations.

numerical control (NC). Refers to the use of computer graphics systems to control and regulate manufacturing tools such as lathes, die cutters, metal bending equipment, flame cutters, etc.

numerical control system. Describes CAD/CAM systems designed to automate a single processing task. Contrast with "process control system."

O

object. A single compiled program ready and available for execution.

object module. A program or group of programs that have been successfully compiled and are ready to be linked into a form suitable for execution.

octal. Describes a numbering system using base eight. Since eight is a power of two, an octal numbering system lends itself very well to the binary processing ability of a computer and is often used in computer graphics systems.

OEM (Original Equipment Manufacturer). Pronounced "oh-ee-em," this term is used to describe turnkey computer system manufacturers who build systems from component parts purchased from a variety of other vendors.

off-line. Describes any operation that occurs independent of the central processor.

offset. 1. Refers to the compensation made by numerically controlled tools to account for the difference in tool length or size from that specified in the numerical control program. 2. Describes the process of defining objects on a graphics system by their relation to and distance from another existing object.

on-line. Describes any processing function that occurs under the control of a central processing unit.

operating system. The lowest level of computer software which functions to control all software dependent processing functions including input, output, scheduling, storage assignment, data management, etc.

operating time. The total time during which a computer graphics system is processing data without system errors or failures.

operation. A general term which describes any single processing task however large or small.

operator. Anyone who uses a computer graphics system to do any processing task. Equivalent to "user."

optical character reader. A device that can scan a page of print, recognize the symbols, and transmit them on-line. Graphics systems that utilize a great deal of textual data are often equipped with these devices.

optical scanner. A device that can view graphic images, sense the light emitted and, thereby, the position of the images, and translate those findings into on-line graphic data comprehensible to a graphics system.

origin. A graphics point or the internal storage address of a point that corresponds to zero on all relevant axes of a coordinate system.

original equipment manufacturer. *See* OEM.

orthographic projection. A projection in which the lines are perpendicular to the plane of projection.

outline. A line along the exterior boundary limits of a graphics entity or file showing its shape and size.

output. Processed data that have been moved or copied from internal storage to a medium that can be viewed directly or taken off-line.

overflow. Output data that exceed the capacity of the system component designated to accept it.

overlay. 1. A clear acetate sheet placed over function keys on which a legend is printed that identifies the function activated by each key. 2. A program execution technique in which the same areas of internal storage are used to run successive segments of the program.

overlay routine. A specially designed computer program that permits other executing programs to be modified or replaced during their execution thereby avoiding total system failures in the case of errors.

overwrite. To record data on top of data previously existing on a given storage area. The old data are thus removed without requiring a separate erase procedure.

P

P and ID (Piping and Instrumentation Design). A standard CAD/CAM applications package used to design pipelines and processing plants.

pad. Any keyboard input device associated with a computer graphics system.

page. 1. A fixed block of data of a previously defined length. 2. The graphic data that can be displayed simultaneously on a cathode-ray tube screen using a specific scale and projection.

paging. 1. The process of dividing data into page blocks. 2. The process of overlaying program segments into internal memory registers.

painting. The process of displaying graphic data on a cathode-ray tube screen.

panning. The horizontal movement of displayed graphic data across a cathode-ray tube screen.

parabola. A graphics entity consisting of a plane curve formed by a conic section taken at an angle parallel to an element of the intersected cone.

parallax. Refers to the apparent displacement in space of the position of an object viewed from two or more different places not in a straight line. Used to permit the calculation of the image of three-dimensional objects displayed on graphic output devices.

parallel. Describes lines or planes in a graphics file that are an equal distance apart at every corresponding point.

parallel processing. Refers to the simultaneous execution of two or more processing operations on a single computer graphics system.

parallel transmission. Refers to simultaneous communications processes conducted by single computer graphics system.

parameter. Input to a computer graphics system that serves to qualify a processing function. All the optional and required information following a graphics system command on the command line.

parametric. Describes the technique by which a line, curve, or surface is defined by equations based on some independent variable. The technique is used often in computer-aided design and manufacturing facilities.

parity bit. A final binary digit appended to a series of such digits and given the value required to make the sum of all the bits either odd or even. When all bytes are either odd or even in value, errors in the system are more easily found.

parity check. A test which determines whether the number of ones or zeros represented by the binary digits of a byte of data is odd or even. Such tests are commonly used to help determine the validity of data.

partitioning. The separation of hardware elements into logic blocks. Usually refers to logic circuits or disk surfaces.

parts explosion. A drawing of all the pieces composing an assembly which illustrates the relation of the pieces to one another.

parts list. A compilation of the names, numbers, and quantities of all pieces used to produce a manufactured item. Most CAD/CAM systems maintain and update such lists automatically during the course of a design and manufacturing process.

parts program. A software program containing the data and instructions necessary to manufacture a part through numerical control operations.

PASCAL (Philips Automatic Sequence Calculator). A high-level programing language often used to write computer graphics application packages.

passive graphics. Refers to any computer graphics operation that transpires automatically and without operator intervention. Sometimes called "noninteractive graphics."

password. Any character string the user must supply to a computer system to gain access to data files or peripheral devices. Passwords are usually part of system security measures.

patch. Fixing a problem by some temporary method in an effort to reduce down time.

patching. A technique for making corrections in a software routine whereby the incorrect instruction is bypassed, control passes to a new area of storage where a new instruction is written, and control passes back to the original routine at a point just beyond the incorrect section.

path. The hierarchy of files through which control passes to find a particular file.

pattern recognition. The identification of geometric shapes in on-line data through a search conducted automatically.

PCB CAD System. A system manufactured by Gerber Scientific Instrument Company to create finished printed circuit board (PCB) artwork from a designer's rough layout.

PEAC.™ A computer-aided design and drafting system produced by Decision Graphics, Inc. The name is an acronym for Planners, Engineers, Architects, and Consultants.

peripheral device. Any hardware component distinct from the central processing unit but controlled by it for use in data input, output, or both.

peripheral node. A node within a network that is used primarily for running peripheral devices rather than interactive software.

Philips Automatic Sequence Calculator. *See* PASCAL.

photoplotter. 1. A device which produces drawings on photosensitive film or glass plate by using an optical exposure head with a light source along with other optical equipment. 2. The name given to a series of photoplotting equipment manufactured by Gerber Scientific Instrument Company.

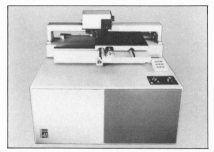 

Photoplotter. A plotter using photosensitive film.

Piping and Instrumentation Design. *See* P and ID.

pixel. The smallest unit available for display on a raster screen, representing a single graphics point. The word is derived from the term "picture element."

PKASO. A printer controller/driver manufactured by Interactive Structures Inc. which provides screen prints, character fonts, and commands, supports many popular matrix printers, and handles both graphic and textual data.

planimeter. A peripheral device that measures the surface area of a plane figure when the perimeter of that figure is traced with a stylus.

Planipad.™ A digitizer with built-in intelligence manufactured by GTCO Corporation. The term derives from "planimeter pad."

plot file. A temporary on-line data file consisting of a copy of graphic information which is used to actually plot a drawing. Usually these files are deleted automatically after the plot is finished.

plotter. A peripheral device that draws figures created with a computer graphics system. Plotters may use a variety of plotting media (paper, vellum, mylar, etc.) on horizontal, vertical, or cylindrical surfaces. They can also employ a variety of pens (ballpoint, drafting pen, felt tip, etc.) and inks.

point. The smallest unit of graphic information representing a single location on a two- or three-dimensional coordinate system.

point identification. A complete, on-line description of a graphics point, including its coordinate location and any special processing functions implied by it.

point set curve. A curve defined by a series of small lines drawn between points.

pointer. On-line data that indicate which data or data file should be processed next during a processing task.

point-to-point. 1. A method of positioning or of identifying a position on a coordinate system. 2. Describes communications between systems in different locations.

polar coordinates. Locations on a coordinate system determined by their angle and vector length from a fixed line.

polling. The technique by which workstations sharing a communications line are queried on a regular basis to determine whether they need access to the line.

port. A connection point on a central processing unit through which a graphics workstation or other device can communicate with the central processing unit directly.

position. The exact location, expressed in mathematical form, of graphic data entered into a coordinate system.

post processor. A software module that reprocesses output data to make them of use to a particular CAD/CAM function, such as a plotter or machine tool.

precision. Refers to the degree of accuracy with which graphic data can be expressed.

pressure sensing pen. A digitizer stylus containing a pressure transducer that detects and transmits writing pressure as z-axis data. Such a pen is manufactured by GTCO Corporation.

Pressure Sensing Pen. A stylus with pressure transducer.

preventive maintenance. Routine cleaning, testing, and adjusting activities designed to prevent equipment failures on a computer graphics system.

primitive. The most basic graphic entities available on a graphics system, such as points, line segments, or characters.

printer. The peripheral device which outputs textual data on paper or photographic material. Sometimes these devices can also output purely graphic data.

printout. The printed or photographic output of a printer. Usually the information is textual rather than graphic.

procedure. A single, defined series of processing steps developed to accomplish a specific task on a graphics system.

process. A series of procedures conducted in an established order to produce a specified result.

process control system. Describes CAD/CAM systems designed to automate continuous, repetitive processing tasks. Contrast with ''numerical control system.''

process plan. A statement revealing exactly which steps are required and in what order for the proper manufacture of a part or assembly.

Producer.℠ The Producer Drafting System is a high-speed, fully automated, turnkey electronic drafting system manufactured by Bausch and Lomb. It has three workstations available where drafters can work concurrently: the Interactive Station, the Digitizer Station, and the Plotter Station.

Producer.℠ A turnkey drafting system manufactured by Bausch and Lomb.

product history data. Refers to all data produced and collected by a computer-aided manufacturing system that relates to the design, development, and manufacture of a specified product. These data may include a series of design iterations, bills of material, engineering specifications, test results, and the like.

production release. Describes a finished product that has been approved for sale and distribution to customers. The term may apply to any component (hardware or software) of a computer graphics system or to the entire system.
Usage: This term differs from ''maintenance release'' in that it denotes a *new* product.

program library. A collection of on-line computer programs available for use on a given graphics system.

project data. Refers to all information available which pertains to the definition of a processing task. Such information usually includes a functional specification or set of design requirements.

prompt. Any message output by a computer graphics system that requires some response from the operator. Systems that display prompts are said to be interactive.

properties. The qualities or attributes associated with an on-line graphics entity or file. Properties are established by the operator during graphic data creation.

protocol. The set of rules governing the communication between the operator and the graphics system or between two or more currently operating processing tasks.

puck. A handheld graphics input device with cross hairs used to pinpoint coordinates on a data tablet or digitizer.

Q

quadrant. One of the rectangles or cubes formed by the axes in a two- or three-dimensional coordinate system.

queue. Refers to a line of processing tasks waiting for access to an output device that must handle the tasks one at a time.

queuing theory. The branch of computer science that deals with creating and disposing of queues. In graphics systems, queuing is concerned primarily with the use of plotters.

R

radix. The base or root of a numbering system. Two is the radix of the binary system; ten is the radix of the decimal system.

random access. Describes data placed in storage at a location unrelated to its proximity to other data or to the speed with which it can later be found and read.

raster. Describes a cathode-ray tube in which a pattern of scanning lines divide the display area into addressable points. Raster display tubes are generally faster and less expensive than vector tubes and are, therefore, gaining popularity for use on CAD/CAM systems.

raster count. The total number of addressable positions on a raster display device.

raster scan. The generation of an image on a display screen made by refreshing the display area line by line.

raster unit. The distance between the midpoints of two adjacent, addressable locations on a raster display screen.

rated speed. The speed at which a graphics system or system component operates under optimal conditions. Actual operating speed is often slower.

raw data. Any data that have not yet been processed by or formatted for a graphics system.

read. To acquire or copy data from one storage device or medium to another. The opposite of "write."
Usage: The standard construction is "read from . . . " whereas the opposite process is usually written "write to . . . . "

real-time. 1. Refers to computation in the central processing unit which occurs while the associated external event is taking place, i.e., a situation in which current processing directly influences a simultaneous, related result. 2. A processing task scheduled not only in terms of priority, but also in terms of the actual time of day.

real-time display. Refers to the output of visible data that occurs simultaneously with the generation of those data by the central processing unit.

real-time operation. Computer controlled processing functions performed at a speed compatible with the simultaneous operation of peripheral mechanical devices.

real-time operations. Describes processing functions that are dependent on events outside the system and, therefore, events which cannot be scheduled for the convenience of the system. Such processing thus proceeds at the pace directed by those outside events or by the simulation of those outside events.

rectangular coordinates system. Same as Cartesian coordinate system. A two- or three-dimensional system in which point locations are determined by their distance from an origin point as measured by two or three axes that form intersecting, perpendicular lines that meet at the point of origin.

refresh. The process of continually redrawing graphic data on a display screen so that the images remain clear and unfaded.

refresh cycle. One complete refresh on a display screen.

register. A hardware device made for the temporary storage of a specified amount of data, usually one byte.

regression testing. Any method of checking maintenance releases of graphics system components to ensure that no new problems have been generated by those releases.

reject. A keyboard character which, when pressed, aborts a pending operation.

relative address. A data storage location defined by its position in relation to some other absolute location rather than in terms of its own absolute location.

relative vector. 1. A directed line with end points which have been defined by their position relative to some other absolute location rather than in terms of their own absolute locations. 2. A line drawn from the last point entered on the graphics system rather than from the origin point.

remote access. Communication between systems or between a system and a peripheral device which occurs by means other than a direct cable hook-up.

remote node. A node within a distributed network that can communicate, through a gateway, with systems outside that network as well as with nodes inside the network.

repaint. The redrawing of an image on an output display device to reflect updated graphic data.

resizing. Refers to the process of scaling a graphics file or entity according to predetermined parameters.

resolution. 1. Refers to the ability of a graphic output device to make distinguishable the individual parts of an object or other images that are very close together in a drawing. 2. The smallest distance that can be processed accurately by a graphics system.

resource. Refers to all sources of processing power which can be brought to bear on a given processing task including hardware and software components, personnel, and previously derived data.

resource sharing. Refers to a situation in which all data, system components, and users can be applied, as needed or as is appropriate, to all processing tasks before the system.

response time. 1. Describes the interval occurring between the moment a processing request is made and the moment that request is enacted by the system. 2. The speed with which a central processing unit can process data.

return. A keyboard character that, when pressed, terminates or executes the command entered just previously. Sometimes the key is also used to transfer control to the next line of a system prompt or to terminate an operator response to a system prompt. Similar to ''carriage return.''

right justified. A series of characters arranged in lines that end flush with the right margin. When applied to numbers it indicates that no significant digits (such as zero) exist to the right of the last digit in the series.

ring. A network of distributed processing systems.

roam. To move a display window around on a display screen.

robotics. Refers to computer controlled machines designed to do repetitive manufacturing tasks formerly done by production line personnel.

rubber banding. A technique for drafting straight lines in desired positions whereby a line is displayed with one end fixed and the other end moveable according to the changing position of a cursor, light pen, or other input device. The technique allows the graphics operator to see how various end points affect the length and angle of a line before that line is entered into a graphics data base.

S

SAGE (Semi-Automatic Ground Environment). Arguably the first use of computer graphics, this system was developed in the mid-1950s by the military to convert radar information into a computer-generated picture.

satellite. Describes a computer graphics minicomputer system with direct communications to a mainframe system.

scalar. The quantity by which graphic data are multiplied or divided to fit some specified size limitations.

scale. 1. *Verb:* to change the size of a graphics file by a specified quantity to make it fit a specified boundary. 2. *Noun:* the quantity by which graphic data are multiplied or divided to fit size limitations.

scan. The automatic, programed examination of data by a graphics system. Such examinations are used to search for specific information or to check the validity of data.

schedule. The process by which a series of jobs are ordered, either by priority level or by the time they are entered, so that they can be processed sequentially and efficiently.

schematic. Describes a graphical representation of the arrangement of some set of hardware components.

scissor. 1. Describes the removal from a graphics file of data lying beyond specified boundaries. Sometimes called ''clipping.'' 2. To divide a drawing or graphics entity into portions that may be viewed independently on a display screen.

scratch pad memory. Temporary high-speed memory used for storing and retrieving small amounts of data quickly.

screen position. The physical location of graphic data displayed on a cathode-ray tube.

scroll. The continuous display (through controlled vertical or horizontal movement) of data on a display screen appearing to move across the screen and out of sight at a steady speed.

sector. The smallest addressable unit of a disk track on a computer graphics system.

segment. 1. *Verb:* to divide into small distinct portions either a computer program or a graphics entity. This allows each portion to be stored or executed separately. 2. *Noun:* a line with defined end points.

Semi-Automatic Ground Environment. *See* SAGE.

sequence number. A number assigned to a graphics entity or file according to the chronological order in which it was entered into the data base.

serial. Pertaining to the arrangement of data or processing tasks in a series. Often refers to the transmission of data through a communication line.

Series 5000 Advanced Graphic Software. A 32-bit graphics software system manufactured by Auto-trol Technology Corporation for use in the architectural, engineering, and construction industries.

Series 7000 Advanced Graphic Software. A 32-bit, menu-driven graphics software system manufactured by Auto-trol Technology Corporation for use in the mechanical design and manufacturing industries.

service bureau. Refers to that group of people employed by a CAD/CAM vendor who respond to customer questions, problems, and who conduct maintenance work.

servomechanism. A feedback system comprising a sensor, amplifier, and motor used to control automatically some mechanical device. Used in numerical control systems.

session. Refers to the period of time during which a graphics system operator works from a terminal at one sitting.

set. Any group of similar or related items of data or groups of data.

shared file. A peripheral device or data file that may be accessed by two or more systems simultaneously.

Shared Resource Manager. A product of Gerber Systems Technology, Inc. that ties their CAD/CAM systems together in a communications network for data management, file management, and peripheral sharing purposes.

sharing. Refers to distributed graphics systems or to graphics systems in communication with one another which have access to some part of the same resources.

Sheet Metal Development. *See* SMD.

shutdown. The termination of electrical power to all or part of the computer graphics system components.

signal. An electrical impulse moving among hardware components in a computer graphics system.

simulation. The representation of all or some part of a system or process for the purpose of predicting its behavior in a real environment.

sketch pad. A working storage area displayed on a cathode-ray tube which permits the operator to add and delete graphic information easily before it is entered into permanent storage.

Sketchpad. A graphics software program written in 1963 by Ivan Sutherland as part of his doctoral dissertation at Massachusetts Institute of Technology. It is regarded by many as the first computer-aided drafting system.

skew. Refers to straight lines in space that are neither parallel nor intersecting.

slewing. Refers to the speed at which numerically controlled machine tools move from one position to another.

slope. Any line, surface, plane, or figure inclined in relation to an axis of a rectangular coordinate system. Most graphics systems can automatically incline graphic entities to any angle designated by a system operator.

SMD. 1. (Sheet Metal Development) is the name of a flat pattern development package manufactured by Gerber Systems Technology, Inc. 2. (Storage Module Drive) is the name sometimes given to independent disk drive units.

smoothing. The process by which sudden fluctuations in value are reduced to make graphic data flow more evenly when output.

software. Computer programs or computer language code.

software portability. Describes computer programs that can be run by more than one central processing unit without modification. As third-party software becomes more prevalent in the graphics industry, portability becomes a more valuable attribute of that software.

solids modeling. Describes a method of displaying solid constructions on a graphics workstation in which they are assigned a distinct color. The entire visible surface of the object is illuminated, giving the construction a solid, three-dimensional appearance. With many graphics systems several solids illuminated in various colors can be displayed simultaneously to illustrate how parts might fit together to form a larger assembly.

spline. One of a series of projections formed along a shaft which fit into corresponding grooves in a hub or other fitting enabling both pieces to rotate together. Spline design is a common application of computer graphics systems.

spooling. The process of placing files in a queue so that they can be sent to an output device in an orderly fashion. In a graphics system, spoolers are often used to queue files competing for plotters or line printers.

stand-alone. Refers to any computer software or any hardware/software system that can operate independently. More specifically, it indicates a program that can execute without benefit of an operating system, or a turnkey computing system that can operate without association with any other computing system.

star networking. Describes a computer graphics system with several remote workstations linked to the same central processing unit.

startup. The process of setting graphics system devices to proper initial conditions and applying appropriate electrical power.

static refresh. A method of creating graphic data stored temporarily in an intelligent workstation rather than in the central processing unit. It permits faster editing of drawings because data need not be transferred back and forth between the workstation and main memory. Static refresh data are usually displayed at half intensity to be distinguished from data permanently stored in the file.

station. An input/output device that permits the operator to accomplish graphics processing tasks and see the result. Synonomous with "workstation."

storage. Refers to any device or medium on which data can be entered, held, and retrieved with a graphics system.

storage module drive. *See* SMD.

storage tube. A cathode-ray tube that not only displays graphic images but saves the data as electrical charges thus preserving the image until the screen is erased. Such tubes do not have to be refreshed and do not flicker.

stroke. 1. Describes textual data stored as graphic entities rather than as American Standard Code for Information Interchange (ASCII) character symbols. On a graphics system, stroked characters can imitate any type face or font size. 2. Any line that makes up part of a graphic entity.

structured programing. Devising an algorithm and writing subsequent software code in such a way that the programing task is reduced to its separate logical steps and each step is addressed by section of the code. In this way the code is made easier to read and simpler to debug.

stylus. A light pen used with a computer graphics system to indicate a cursor position or data point.

Summagrid. A large, high resolution digitizer with power lift stand manufactured by Summagraphics Corporation.

Summagrid. A large-scale, high-resolution
digitizer with stand.

Supergrid. A digitizer manufactured by Summagraphics Corporation which features multi-bus compatible controllers, remote programmability, translucent, opaque, or rear projection screens, and a variety of cursor and stylus options.

Supergrid. A high-resolution, high accuracy digitizer.

surface of revolution. Refers to the figure resulting from the rotation of a curve around a fixed axis set at a specified angle.

swapping. Refers to the process of temporarily exchanging one executing program for another in the central processing unit for the purpose of maximizing processing efficiency.

swim. Describes a situation in which the images displayed on a cathode-ray tube screen move due to some hardware instability or defect.

symbol table. A group of on-line graphic symbols that are used frequently in the course of running some computer graphics application. Copies of the symbols are then created automatically as needed.

Symbolic Data Entry. *See* SYMDE.

SYMDE (SYMbolic Data Entry). An input device used on Gerber Systems Technology Inc. CAD/CAM systems which allows users to prepare up to ninety-nine pages of sixty-three symbols each for graphic symbology recognition and data entry.

SYMDE (Symbolic Data Entry). A SYMDE tablet on which graphic symbols are displayed.

symmetry. Refers to the correspondence, equivalence, or identity among graphic entities or parts of entities in a graphics file or data base. Creating symmetrical drawings on a graphics system is often facilitated through such automated functions as copying, scaling, mirroring, and duplicating.

syntax. The set of rules governing the use of a particular programing language or program statement.

sysgen. *See* system generation.

system. 1. A group of components working together to perform some task. Refers to personnel, hardware, software, or any combination. 2. Refers to all hardware and software components that compose a single computer graphics installation.

system generation (sysgen). The process of building a software system from the operating system up, linking the pieces, and testing it to be sure there are no errors. Often used to describe this process when it has been automated, i.e., when one software system is used to build another.

system integration. Refers to a complete computer graphics system design in which all hardware and software components have been made to perform complementary functions.

system log. A record of all tasks conducted by a graphics system along with various descriptive information such as who the operator was, what time the tasks ran, how long they took, command input, and the like.

system manager. The person responsible for allocating the resources of a computer graphics system. This person is also often responsible for system maintenance, repair, and security.

system utilization. The total amount of time a graphics system is used for productive purposes. A rate of system efficiency.

T

table. A group of data arranged according to some stated, logical rationale.

table lookup. A search through a data table or series of tables for items having some specific characteristic. Often used on graphics systems to update bills of material.

tablet. A small digitizer made for use on a desk top or on a work surface next to a graphics workstation. Often such digitizers are low-resolution and are used solely to position a cursor on the graphics display screen of a workstation.

tag. A textual identifier associated with a graphics symbol in a graphics data base, enabling it to be easily identified or modified.

telecommunications. Pertains to the transmission of data over large distances.

Tell-A-Graf.™ A business graphics application program for producing line, bar, and pie charts as well as text pages. Manufactured by Integrated Software Systems Corporation.

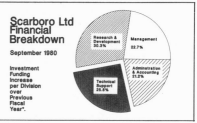

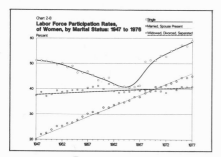
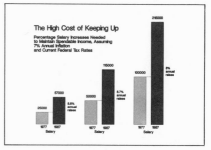

Tell-A-Graf.™ A business graphics software package for producing charts and text.

terminal. An input/output device with which a graphics operator can access and operate a graphics system.

text editor. A software program designed to allow an operator to create and modify textual data on-line by means of various commands.

texture. Describes the quality and accuracy of vectors displayed on the output devices of a graphics system.

The Data Connection.™ An integrated portfolio of software tools manufactured by Integrated Software Systems Corporation and designed to solve data acquisition, analysis, and management problems that commonly occur when outputting graphics data to its Tell-A-Graf™ graphics software package.

three-dimensional. Describes graphic information presented with visual aspects representing three physical extents: height, width, and depth.

throughput. A measure of the rate at which data input to a graphics system is processed and output.

thumbwheel. A device for positioning an input cursor and consisting of a rotatable wheel which controls the movement of that cursor in one axis. Normally, thumbwheels are found in pairs, one controlling vertical cursor movement, the other horizontal movement.

time slice. 1. The interval of time during which a central processing unit is engaged with a single program. 2. The time between the moment a program is swapped into the central processing unit and the moment it is swapped out.

time-sharing. Describes the use of a computer system by more than one process simultaneously.

tooling. The cutting and shaping instruments and the functions of these instruments in the manufacture of a product or product part.

topology. Refers to the hardware configuration of a computer graphics system. Most often used in the context of a computer graphics system network and the arrangement of the various nodes.

track. 1. *Verb:* to follow or record the moving position of a cursor, stylus, or other input device. 2. *Noun:* a single line of data on a disk surface forming a concentric circle around the central spindle and along which data are written to be read later from a single head position.

tracking symbol. The small graphics figure on a display device that represents the position of the cursor. A cross, point, or lighted square are the symbols most commonly used.

translate. To transform data from one form to another for use in different processing tasks. The translation of graphic data in internal storage to a form acceptable to an output device.

tube. A cathode-ray tube used to display graphic data.

turnkey system. A complete, integrated, and tested computer graphics system. A graphics system in which the vendor is responsible for producing, integrating, delivering, installing, testing, and maintaining all hardware and software components.

two-dimensional. Describes graphic information presented with visual aspects representing two physical extents: height and width.

U

UltraGraf.™ An interactive, three-dimensional computer-aided design graphics workstation manufactured by Lundy Electronics and Systems, Inc.

UltraGraf.™ A graphics workstation manufactured by Lundy Electronics and Systems, Inc.

update. To modify a graphics file and make it reflect more recent information.

upgrade. 1. *Noun:* describes an enhancement or other improvement to a graphics system component. 2. *Verb:* to apply an enhancement or other improvement to a component of an existing graphics system.

user. Any person authorized to operate any aspect of a computer graphics system. Very often such authorization comes by means of a password or other unique identifier known to a system security mechanism.

utilities. Those programs that provide special processing functions which aid graphic activities but are not themselves graphic functions. These functions include dumps, saves, listings, compiling, binding, copying, deleting, initializing, and the like.

V

vector. 1. A directed quantity described by its magnitude and direction. In computer graphics systems, line segments are vectors defined by their two end points. 2. Describes a cathode-ray tube on which graphic data is represented by lines drawn from point to point rather than by illumination of a series of contiguous positions, as on a raster cathode-ray tube.

vector generation. The creation of lines by a computer graphics system.

verification. The act of authenticating the validity or accuracy of data. This is often done on a computer graphics system as data are first entered, thus ensuring the integrity of the on-line data base.

vertical axis. The y axis in a Cartesian coordinate system.

vertical spacing. Refers to the actual space or to the number of characters or symbols that will fit in the space between two points arranged vertically.

Videograph.℠ A short-turnaround, short-burst graphics software system for video and slide production produced by Xiphias.

viewing angle. The angle formed above or below the right angle formed when the viewer faces the center of the display area.

viewing area. The total exposed display face of a cathode-ray tube that can be seen by the station user.

viewing distance. The distance between the system user and the output device s/he is observing.

viewpoint. That position on a display screen where output graphic data first appears as a graphics file is output.

virtual memory. An area available for data storage which appears to a program as hardware, but is actually space made available by a software swapping mechanism.

W

wetzel. A picture element added to the image on a cathode-ray tube to improve the sharpness of the display. Coined through a combination of the German verb "wetzen," meaning "to sharpen or hone," and the graphics term "pixel," meaning "picture element."

window. A defined area within a display screen that can be used as a working area. A number of windows may be active simultaneously on one display screen. The windows may be on discrete parts of the screen or may overlay one another.

wireframe. Describes a method of outputting solid constructions on a graphics system in which a skeleton of that solid is formed by lines representing all edges, surfaces, and stress points, or by lines drawn at regular intervals around a three-dimensional entity. These lines have the cumulative effect of illustrating the solid shape of the construction.

word. In a computer, a sequence of binary digits (bits) that is treated as a single unit and can be stored in one core memory location. Sometimes termed a "byte."

working storage. The temporary storage available on an intelligent workstation in which data currently being created are stored before being entered into the permanent graphics data base.

workstation. An input/output device assigned to a graphics system operator from which s/he can access and operate all system software and peripherals. A workstation usually consists of a display screen, a keyboard, and a working surface. The workstation may also have limited intelligence, the result of microcomputer chips mounted inside the chassis. Nevertheless, the workstation is dependent upon a host central processing unit.

wraparound. The continuation of a processing or display operation from the last addressable memory location or the last display position on a central processing unit back to the first location or position.

write. To record data on a storage device or medium. The opposite of "read."
Usage: The standard construction is "write to . . ." whereas the opposite process is usually "read from. . . ."

X-Y-Z

x axis. The reference line of a rectangular coordinate system used by computer graphics systems to determine horizontal distance and positions.

y axis. The reference line of a rectangular coordinate system used by computer graphics systems to determine vertical distance and positions.

z axis. The reference line of a rectangular coordinate system used by computer graphics systems to determine extents of depth and the position of points in that dimension.

z-clipping. Refers to the process of specifying the depth limits of a three-dimensional drawing which determine the positions beyond which all data become invisible when that drawing is displayed. This process is used as a viewing aid when displaying very complex or detailed drawings.

zero. The origin point from which all absolute vectors are defined in a coordinate system.

zoom. The process by which the perspective on a displayed graphics file moves rapidly closer or farther from the operator.